The Past in the Present

Southern Literary Studies
Louis D. Rubin, Jr., Editor

THOMAS
DANIEL
YOUNG

The Past in the Present

A Thematic Study of Modern Southern Fiction

Louisiana State University Press
Baton Rouge and London

Designer: Patricia Douglas Crowder
Typeface: VIP Sabon
Typesetter: LSU Press
Printer and Binder: Thomson-Shore, Inc.

LIBRARY OF CONGRESS CATALOGING IN PUBLICATION DATA

Young, Thomas Daniel, 1919–
   The past in the present

   (Southern literary studies)
   1. American fiction—Southern States—History
and criticism.   2. American fiction—20th century
—History and criticism.   I. Title.   II. Series.
PS261.Y6   813'.52'09   80–24074
ISBN 0–8071–0768–9·

   The author gratefully acknowledges permission to quote from the
following:
   William Faulkner, *The Unvanquished*, copyright © 1965, Vintage
Books, by Random House, Inc.
   Robert Penn Warren, *All the King's Men*, copyright © 1946 by Har-
court Brace Jovanovich, Inc.
   Eudora Welty, *The Optimist's Daughter*, copyright © 1972 by
Random House, Inc.
   Flannery O'Connor, *The Complete Stories*, copyright © 1964, 1965
by the Estate of Mary Flannery O'Connor; *Mystery and Manners*, copy-
right © 1957, 1961, 1963, 1964, 1966, 1967, 1969 by the Estate of Mary
Flannery O'Connor; copyright © 1962 by Flannery O'Connor; copyright
© 1961 by Farrar, Straus and Cudahy, Inc.; *The Habit of Being*, copy-
right © 1979 by Regina O'Connor.
   Walker Percy, *The Moviegoer*, copyright © 1961, by Alfred A. Knopf,
Inc.
   John Barth, *The End of the Road*, copyright © 1958, 1967 by John
Barth. Reprinted by permission of Doubleday, Inc.

For Daniel Allen

With the War of 1914–1918, the South reentered the world—but gave a backward glance as it stepped over the border: that backward glance gave us the Southern renascence, a literature conscious of the past in the present.

Allen Tate, "The New Provincialism"

Contents

Preface

In his *The Dispossessed Garden* Professor Lewis P. Simpson writes most provocatively on what we have come to refer to as the Southern Literary Renaissance. "This flowering of literature in fiction and criticism, and to a somewhat lesser extent in poetry," he believes, "rivals the nineteenth-century New England efflorescence." The basic reason for this revival of interest in literature in the South, Simpson continues, was that about 1920 some southern writers, now recognized as among the most important of their generation, "inaugurated a struggle to comprehend the nature of memory and history." They were specifically interested in attempting to demonstrate the "redemptive meaning of the classical-Christian past in its bearing on the present." The southern writers, then, born in the last decade of the last century and first decade of this one, and whose best work appeared in the period between the two wars, were primarily engaged in a struggle to find "the meaning of the past," to discover or reconstruct some viable relationship to their tradition.[1]

As illuminating as this insight is, it requires expansion and demonstration if it is to assist as much as it might in understanding not only the complex and highly subjective literary expressions of the period but in providing some indication of why the modern southern writers wrote what and how

---

1 Lewis P. Simpson, *The Dispossessed Garden* (Athens: University of Georgia Press, 1975), 70.

they did. Whereas the past meant something quite specific to each writer, its meaning varied a great deal from one artist to another. The past that Donald Davidson wished to recover, quite literally, was that of the Jeffersonian South. Although both Allen Tate and John Crowe Ransom sought a society that gave appropriate homage to established traditions, the nature and function of these traditions were matters upon which they did not completely agree. Some of William Faulkner's fiction can be most profitably read, it would seem, in the light of Ransom's much quoted statement that the importance of religion to modern man lies in its ritual, not in its dogma.

If one accepts this thesis, it will add a dimension to the attitude of those critics who have insisted that the best literature of the modern South came out of a society whose members believed the nature of metaphysical reality was explained only by Christian doctrine, that the post-World War I southern society was one of believers, one with faith in and relationship to an omnipotent God who rules over a universe to a small part of which human beings precariously cling. A part of my purpose in the pages that follow, then, is, first of all, to present some of the different views of the nature and function of tradition held by the most significant of the writers who contributed to the renaissance. Then to demonstrate the importance of a belief in ritual, ceremony, pageantry, and manners in a world from which the gods have disappeared.

After this introductory chapter, there are six chapters, each one treating a different novel, or in the case of Flannery O'Connor, a selection of her short stories. The first two chapters discuss two novels—William Faulkner's *The Unvanquished* and Allen Tate's *The Fathers*—both published in the same year and both treating, with significant differences, the importance of codes of manners, ceremonies, and ritualistic behavior in a traditional society. There follows an examination of Robert Penn Warren's *All the King's Men*, in which, as Walter Sullivan has pointed out, "the old order and the new collide, and the old codes of conduct, the old institutions, and the old heroes are destroyed."[2] More pertinent to my theme, however, is Warren's view of the relation of past and present, the nature of metaphysical reality, as presented in his best-known novel. The religious views of Jack Burden, Warren's protagonist, seem to rely little on faith in Christian doctrine; instead they are, to use Pascal's phrase, "the religion of the philosophers and scholars." Eudora Welty's *The Optimist's Daughter* vividly exposes the means by which a sense of community and life grounded in ritualistic behavior becomes obsolete. Flannery O'Connor is the only modern or contemporary southern writer whose fiction is firmly anchored in the tenets of Christianity, in what she calls the "God of Abraham, Isaac, and Jacob" and not the one created by "philosophers and scholars." O'Connor's Christian conviction, as I have said, makes her unique among her contemporaries, whose work seems to prove the validity of Ransom's statement that for the modern writer "religion is an institution existing for the sake of its ritual, rather than . . . for the sake of its doctrines."[3] This is one of the basic assumptions around which the present study is developed.

After World War II this Southern Renaissance, Simpson believes, entered a second phase, one in which the most significant writers attempted "to record the breakdown of the endeavor in reconstruction and to suggest, moreover, that the process of memory and history within the literary mind . . . cannot be halted; that the inauguration of any attempt to establish a new literary covenant is futile."[4] These writers were attempting to find some acceptable relationship between themselves and an apparently absurd universe. Through examina-

---

2 Walter Sullivan, *A Requiem for the Renascence* (Athens: University of Georgia Press, 1976), 25.
3 John Crowe Ransom, *The World's Body* (Baton Rouge: Louisiana State University Press, 1968), 43.
4 Simpson, *The Dispossessed Garden*, 71.

tion of two typical novels of the period this study attempts to demonstrate that the literature produced in the South has lost its unique regional flavor, those characteristics that made it distinct from the work produced by writers in other sections of the country. Like contemporary writers the world over, the most important southern novelists, poets, and short-story writers whose best work has appeared since World War II have abandoned the search for a meaningful tradition; instead they have found that the only search that can fully command their attention and engage their talents can be defined in existential terms alone. With the abandonment of the struggle to find a meaningful relationship to the region's traditional heritage and to bring the ritualistic aspects of that heritage into modern culture, the writers of the South lost the impetus that produced a distinctively different literature, and the renaissance was over.

One last statement should be made, I think, about the contemporary southern writers, of whom I consider two— Walker Percy and John Barth. Not unlike their counterparts elsewhere, these two writers base their speculations upon the premise that "existence precedes essence" in order to try to establish some acceptable relation to a seemingly indifferent and incomprehensible universe. Even with this common beginning, however, they arrive at different conclusions. Percy's Binx Bolling sets out to *know* what Ransom calls the "common actuals" of the sensuous world around him, he forms lasting personal relationships with others who inhabit this realm with him, and proceeds to Kierkegaard's religious realm. From a fear of becoming "an anyone living anywhere," he has become convinced of his individual being, a person of dignity and stature. Barth's Jacob Horner, however, is affected with "Cosmopsis"; he is aware only of universals, not of particulars. With what Tate calls "the long view of history" or what Ransom insists is the modern tendency to "abstract through subtraction," Horner remains convinced that life is a meaningless drama and living merely a matter of playing a series of worthless roles; therefore he has no realization of self, society, or God. Nothingness is all.

The novels discussed in this study are not intended to represent the quality of the fiction produced in the South during the past half century. Surely *The Unvanquished* is not Faulkner's best; and I do not suggest by including here Tate's *The Fathers*, a poet's only novel, that it is a great work of art (although I think it is of very high quality). All of the works of fiction included in this book, and my discussions of those works, are intended to serve one purpose: to demonstrate the validity of my thesis.

Acknowledgments

Many have assisted in the preparation of this book. My greatest debt is to the scholars who have preceded me in studying the writers of the modern South, particularly Lewis P. Simpson and Louis D. Rubin. I should also like to thank George Core, Floyd Watkins, and Thomas D. Young, Jr., who read the manuscript and made many valuable suggestions. John Hindle and Frederick L. Hull assisted me in many ways. Alberta Martin and Louise Durham typed the many versions this manuscript went through in reaching its present stage.

I owe a special debt to Martha L. Hall of the Louisiana State University Press, whose imaginative and careful editing has improved almost every page of this book.

Most of all I am grateful to my wife, Arlease Lewis Young, whose help and encouragement made the writing of this book almost always a pleasure.

The Past in the Present

I Memory and History: The Nature and Function of Tradition

Although their views of the meaning of the past covered a fairly broad spectrum of opinion, nearly all southern novelists whose writings have appeared since World War I have been opposed to the emphasis modern society has placed on technology and consumer economics. This emphasis they have seen as a debasement of man's humanity and as conducive to the creation of an intellectual climate in which classical-Christian values cannot exist. Central to the work of the writers whose best work appeared between the two wars is the "effort to achieve . . . the meaning of the South in terms of the classical-Christian historical order of being." This struggle helped to bring into existence some of the most enduring fiction of the twentieth century; much of this fiction has one common characteristic, the authors' disinclination to believe that the problems confronting modern men can be solved by science (including technology), the social sciences, or industrial capitalism. They are not convinced that man has, or ever will have, the knowledge to change the fundamental order of being. Most writers of the modern South insist that man does not have the power to change the basic structure of the universe, despite the insistence of some social planners that man is evolving toward the time when perfect human beings will have developed a perfect social order. The most important modern southern writers contend that man lives in a continuum of time and will never know how the story of human existence will end.[1]

One of the recurring themes in modern southern literature is the struggle between the values that have long supported Western European civilization and those held by modern gnosticism. "Our total purpose," Donald Davidson says of himself and his fellow Agrarians, "was to seek the image of the South which we could cherish with high conviction and to give it, wherever we could, the finality of art." Convinced that environmental factors are not the chief means of determining the character of a society, these writers sought to restore "some commanding image" of the South's past in "those forms, fictional, poetical, or dramatic, that have the character of myth." Since these presentations rest firmly on belief, they attempt to breed belief in others, and since they were mythopoeic in origin, they, unlike arguments, are unanswerable and in themselves are "fulfilled and complete."[2]

Davidson's conception of the kind of society he wished to reconstitute was one that establishes and then maintains "with markable loyalty the institutions that flow from common adherence to democratic principles." The social order he would revive was one that was "stable, religious, more rural than urban, and politically conservative." In such a society "[f]amily, blood-kinships, clanship, folk-ways, custom, [and] community fulfill" needs that in a nontraditional society are inadequately and expensively met by government agencies.[3]

The important southern writers between the two wars,

1 Lewis P. Simpson, *The Dispossessed Garden* (Athens: University of Georgia Press), 75, 76, 78 *passim*.
2 Donald Davidson, *Southern Writers in the Modern World* (Athens: University of Georgia Press, 1958), 60, 61. Although his one novel was never published, Donald Davidson as teacher and thinker influenced many of the important southern writers of his day.
3 Donald Davidson, *Still Rebels, Still Yankees and Other Essays* (Baton Rouge: Louisiana State University Press, 1972), 207.

with the exception of Thomas Wolfe, Davidson argues, had a unified view of life and did not suffer from the common malady of the time, the separation of thought and feeling. Such writers as Faulkner, Ransom, and Tate not only had an "endless store of subject matter" but they were aware of the form in which that subject matter should be expressed. If the writer comes from a traditional society, Davidson writes, unless he is corrupted, as Wolfe, Erskine Caldwell, and Carson McCullers were, he "will act as a whole person in all his acts, including the literary acts."[4] In Ransom's words, he can both fathom and perform his nature.

2

Allen Tate never seriously considered a literal reconstruction of the antebellum South, according to Louis D. Rubin, Jr., although his interest in that society was as profound as Davidson's. Tate was, most of all, concerned with finding out who he was and where he belonged in the Waste Land of the Northeast where he had gone to live and write in the mid-1920s.[5] In an essay entitled the "Last Days of the Charming Lady" (1925), he points to the rigid social order of the Old South, as well as to its charm, but he also says the modern southerner "has no tradition of ideas, no consciousness of moral or spiritual values." Soon after his essay was written Tate spent a year in Europe, still searching for a vantage from which he could view his ethical and aesthetic position in the world. Then he became involved in *I'll Take My Stand* (1930), to which he contributed an essay on southern religion. This symposium, Tate later wrote, he considered not a defense of the South but a call for the return of religious humanism.

By the mid-1930s Tate was lamenting the absence of a profession of letters in the South and proclaiming that the lit-

4 *Ibid.*, 176.
5 Louis D. Rubin, Jr., *The Wary Fugitives: Four Poets and the South* (Baton Rouge: Louisiana State University Press, 1978), 102.

erary output of the section would be scant until that region, like France, recognized the value of literature to the state. He had come to see, however, that the "southern" attitude was different from the dominant American one, which he defined as a "social point of view," one that requires not a literature of "conviction and experience" but one supported by "statistical survey." Had the antebellum planter class not been obsessed with politics, a profession of letters might have developed in the South because the pre-Civil War South was a traditional society, one noted for its amiability and consideration of manners, one that believed in a "Code of Honor." It was a social order centered in the patriarchal family, the "man on the land." It propagated a culture fostering a "unified sense of its own destiny," one which believed that man lived on both "bread and sentiment." Above all, it demonstrated its conviction that "the concrete forms of the social and religious life are the assimilating structure of society." [6]

The identifying characteristic of the society of the Old South, he continues, was its "comparative stability," its limited "acquisitive impulse," its "preference for human relationships." The greatest inadequacy of this society, he insists, was that it never created a "fitting religion." The religion developed in the South, as well as in the North, was not the kind needed to support a feudal society, which the antebellum southern society was. It was a religion intended to further the Jamestown project, a capitalistic enterprise intent on the wholesale exploitation of nature in order to advance trade as an end in itself.[7]

The modern southern writer, Tate warned in 1935, despite the unifying tradition that lies behind him, is "perilously close to losing his identity and becoming merely a modern

6 Allen Tate, *Essays of Four Decades* (New York: William Morrow, 1968), 521–23.
7 Allen Tate, "Remarks on the Southern Religion," in *I'll Take My Stand* by Twelve Southerners (Baton Rouge: Louisiana State University Press, 1977), 166–67.

writer," for he is losing the "Southern feeling" and retaining merely a southern subject, which he writes about as an outsider with some "novelty of technique" and a "smart superior attachment." For this reason, Tate warned more than forty years ago, the southern dominance of American fiction is a passing phenomenon: "The Southern novelist has left his mark upon the age; but it is of the age. From the peculiarly historical consciousness of the Southern writer has come good work of a special order; but the focus of this consciousness is quite temporary." Ten years later he proclaimed: "the Renaissance is over. . . . Today the motive behind our action is not, is this right, but will this work?" The regional consciousness, that habit of men in a certain locality which "influences them to certain patterns of thought handed down to them by their ancestors" is now subsumed in what he calls the "new provincialism," one which is limited in time if not in space. The holder of this modern view, northerner and southerner alike, thinks the "present moment is unique." He has cut himself off from the past and without the fund of "traditional wisdom," he "approaches the simplest problem as if no one had ever heard of it before. . . . The provincial man, locked in the present, lives by chance." Man today is committed to chance solutions of "problems" that seem unique only because he has forgotten his own nature. The writers whose best work appeared between the two world wars wrote a distinct kind of literature because they took the South they knew, and what they could learn of its past, and discovered that it was a region of special characteristics, one that offered "as an imaginative subject the plight of human beings as it had been and will doubtless continue to be, here and in other parts of the world." [8]

After World War I, to repeat Tate's well-known statement, the "South reentered the world—but gave a backward

8 Tate, *Essays of Four Decades*, 533, 539–45.

glance as it stepped over the border: that backward glance gave us the Southern renascence, a literature conscious of the past in the present." This double focus—Tate's version of Faulkner's "The past isn't dead; it isn't even past"—allowed the writer of his generation, to view his region as one possessing a traditional society, one in which "the way of life" and the "livelihood of man" are the same. In such a society the way one makes his living strongly affects his way of life. Man is so situated that he can "form a definite conception" of his human role. He knows what he is. He is able to perform at all levels of human existence.[9]

Many writers of the modern South believe that a traditional society can be identified by the kind of human beings produced by that society.[10] In this kind of society, too, man still possessed what Tate calls a "historical imagination." He could still imagine himself in the role of a historical hero, even if he could no longer see himself "under the control of a tutelary deity." He could measure himself, his actions and aspirations, by the standards of Cato, if not of Apollo.[11] One characteristic of the member of a nontraditional society is the inclination to attempt to reduce the concrete particularities of the sensuous world to an abstract statement. Tate believes that T. S. Eliot's contrast between the traditions of the past, as represented by the decor in the room where the lady in *The Waste Land* sits, and the pointless game of chess—a deliber-

9 *Ibid.*, 545, 547–50.
10 Andrew Lytle argues that the southern writers who grew up in the second and third decades of this century differed from those of a generation or two later because they were members of a society with traditions old enough "to have roots." The writers who grew up in such a society had a "coherent view of life." For this was a "historic moment everywhere in the Western world," the latter part of the nineteenth and the first part of the twentieth century. This time in the South "was the last moment of equilibrium . . . the last time a man could know who he was. Or where he was from. It was the last time a man, without having to think, could say what was right and what was wrong." Stability and order, which permitted man to fill his moral role as human being through a suprarational process, was Lytle's idea of a traditional society. (*The Hero with the Private Parts* [Baton Rouge: Louisiana State University Press, 1966], 173.)
11 Tate, *Essays of Four Decades*, 551.

ately abstract and intellectual exercise—is a dramatic presentation of this aspect of modernity. Contemporary man, like the lady in the poem, is surrounded by the grandeurs of the past; yet he cannot participate in them. His is not a traditional society, one able to pass on to the next generation what it received from the previous one. In the present age, it naturally follows, there has been a deterioration of, and a general disregard for, manners, rituals, rites, codes and morals; therefore man can only expend his energy in violence. Dominated by rational positivism, he has lost the high myth of religion— which should be "in conviction immediate, direct, overwhelming" (the phrase is Tate's)—and he no longer possesses even the lower myth of historical imagination; he can no longer fulfill his human role. His life is merely a series of pragmatic conquests. That man is capable of acting at a level higher than that at which he spends the bulk of his time is a basic concern in much of the fiction written from 1925 to 1950, but other considerations dominate most of that which comes later. The presence of attitudes, such as those prevalent in the critical writings of Allen Tate, in the best fiction written between the two world wars accounts not only for its distinctly classical tone but it also contributes many of its basic thematic attitudes.

Tate contrasts, for example, the contemporary view of society with the traditional attitudes that operated in the small Kentucky community in which he grew up. In his youth, he says, his neighbors placed great emphasis on land and material property, on a definite place, and very little on money. If people were not *where* they ought to be, they could not be *who* they ought to be and the place became "dominated by a sense of dislocated external relations," a state very much like that which exists for Horace Benbow in *Sanctuary* (1931) or for the Compson family in *The Sound and the Fury* (1929). In the Civil War, Tate insists, Robert E. Lee fought for a definite concrete place, his home community, which he could not "abstract into fragments" as his modern counterparts could. A nontraditional man in his position would have "tossed his loyalties back and forth," come out with an abstraction called Justice and fought for the Federal Union, if he fought at all.

Much of contemporary American literature, in the South as elsewhere, is a literature of no specific place. Both Walker Percy and John Barth, for example, would deny the significance of geography. Jacob Horner is, in Percy's phrase, "an anyone living anywhere" and the place where Binx Bolling resides is essentially characterless, as much like dozens of other suburbs of middle-sized American cities as industrial capitalism can make it. In fact Jacob Horner's psychic imbalance may be the result of his reducing to abstractions the physical environment in which he lives. According to Frederick J. Hoffman, "The values of place in literature (as distinguished from scene, which is merely unindividualized space) come from its being fixed but also associated with neighboring spaces that share a history, some communicable tradition and idiom, in terms of which a personality can be identified." [12] Both Binx Bolling from *The Moviegoer* (1961) and Jacob Horner from John Barth's *The End of the Road* (1967) suffer from the "new provincialism." They belong to no specific place, and are caught up in the present moment. Unlike Bayard Sartoris from Faulkner's *The Unvanquished* (1938) and Lacy Buchan from Tate's *The Fathers* (1938), they feel no sense of loyalty to tradition, nor do they attach any values to the formal and ceremonial attitudes toward the human condition. As Faulkner suggests in *Go Down, Moses* (1942), and as the contributors to *I'll Take My Stand* (1930) argue repeatedly, a disregard for the significance of place initiates a meaningless exploitation of nature and an utter disregard for the ceremo-

12 Frederick J. Hoffman, "The Sense of Place," in *South: Modern Southern Literature in Its Cultural Setting*, ed. Louis D. Rubin, Jr., and Robert D. Jacobs (Garden City: Doubleday, 1961), 60.

nies through which man can live at peace with the natural forces of the universe. Such is the nontraditional view. To the traditionalist, however, land is a tangible concrete place that evokes certain feelings in those who have a proper respect for it. Land is not a place, as Lytle has noted, where one grows wealthy; it is a place where one grows corn. On it, as Isaac McCaslin learns, man can live fruitfully only if he is bound by the agreements he has made with nature.

Eudora Welty has written forcefully about the function of place in her fiction and in that of her contemporaries. Place, she writes, helps the writer to focus his vision, assists him in creating an illusion of reality, in convincing his reader that the concrete particularities presented in fiction are not a lie but are indeed the world's reality or, in Ransom's view, the body of the world. "It seems plain," Welty insists, "that the art that speaks most clearly, explicitly, directly, and passionately from its place of origin will remain the longest understood. It is through place that we put out roots . . . but where these roots reach toward . . . is the deep and running vein, eternal and consistent and everywhere purely itself, that feeds and is fed by the human understanding." [13] To see again how so basic an idea—one found in so much important modern fiction—has been questioned by contemporary southern writers, one need only recall Binx Bolling's dilemma. Despite Walker Percy's public expressions of regard for the quality of Welty's art, Binx is convinced that trying to find one's roots in a fixed tradition of the past will seriously interfere with his "search," his attempt to find some acceptable relationship between himself and an absurd world. A sense of belonging to a specific place, and of having definite feelings toward it, is an essential ingredient in the credo of the traditionalist.

Tate argues that the southern writer of his generation, un-

13 Eudora Welty, *The Eye of the Story* (New York: Random House, 1977), 132.

like those of previous generations, was able to employ the past in a unique manner because he became aware of himself and his relationship to his tradition through a changing mode of the imagination. "The traditional Southern mode of discourse"—the one common in the antebellum South—presupposed "somebody at the other end silently listening: it is the rhetorical mode. Its historical rival is the dialectical mode, or the give and take between two minds, even if one mind, like the mind of Socrates, prevail in the end." This change in the southern imagination, which is responsible for much of the best writing from the novelists and poets of his generation, occurred because "the South not only reentered the world with the first World War; it looked around and saw for the first time since about 1830 that the Yankees were not to blame for everything." [14] Although it looks now like a simple discovery, one can see that it was the internal conflict within authors like Warren, Tate and Faulkner—their attempts to identify their relationships to their tradition, to find the "past in the present" through their associations with a specific place at a particular time—that inspired the discovery and creation of what Malcolm Cowley has called the southern legend, a mythopoeic tale of defeat and heroic frustration that the best writers of the generation between the two wars "converted into a universal myth of the human condition."

Cowley's version of this southern myth, though we shall see it differs at some points from that of Tate, should make evident the legend—the tradition—to which the creative imaginations of a generation of southern writers reacted. It was one fixed in time and place:

> The Deep South was settled partly by aristocrats like the Sartoris clan and partly by new men like Colonel Sutpen. Both types of planters were determined to establish a lasting social order on the land they had

14 Tate, *Essays of Four Decades*, 583, 592.

seized from the Indians (that is, to leave sons behind them). They had the virtue of living single-mindedly by a fixed code; but there was an inherent guilt in their "design," their way of life; it was slavery that put a curse on the land and brought about the Civil War. After the War was lost, partly as a result of their own mad heroism . . . they tried to restore "the design" by other methods. But they no longer had the strength to achieve more than a partial success, even after they had freed their land from the carpetbaggers who followed the Northern armies. As time passed, moreover, the men of the old order found that they had Southern enemies too: they had to fight against a new exploiting class descended from the landless whites of slavery days. In this struggle between the clan of Sartoris and the unscrupulous tribe of Snopes, the Sartorises were defeated in advance by a traditional code that kept them from using the weapons of the enemy. As a price of victory, however, the Snopeses had to serve the mechanized civilization of the North, which was morally impotent in itself, but which with the aid of its Southern retainers, ended by corrupting the Southern nation.[15]

Despite its usefulness in revealing the relationship among Faulkner's interconnecting series of novels, this statement of the thematic concerns lying behind the Yoknapatawpha fiction has been criticized as being too restrictive. Warren has said that the thread holding the Yoknapatawpha cycle together is not the deterioration of the South but the falling apart of Western European civilization, and Tate's explanation for the decay of the antebellum southern civilization, as we shall see, differs somewhat from that which Cowley attributes to Faulkner. Others have commented on Cowley's failure to emphasize the amorality of the code of ethics under which the Snopeses act, and Cleanth Brooks has suggested that Cowley's distinction between the "Sartoris clan" and the "tribe of Snopes" is not sharp enough.

So that we can understand better such discussions as that between Bayard and Drusilla in *The Unvanquished* or the difference between Colonel Sartoris' actions after the Civil

15 Malcolm Cowley, "Introduction," *The Portable Faulkner* (New York: Viking, 1946), 14.

War and those of Colonel Sutpen, Brooks discusses the concept of aristocracy that existed in the antebellum South. He argues that "the code of values and general outlook" of Sutpen differed considerably from those of the other planters in Yoknapatawpha County. Sutpen was a nontraditional man; he was unaware of the demands placed upon a man in a position of leadership in the society to which he belonged. To indicate the basic difference between Sutpen and his fellow planters, Brooks seeks support from two eminent historians —Eugene Genovese and C. Vann Woodward. Despite the fact that most southern planters were of plebeian origin, as Sutpen was, their basic attitudes toward certain fundamental questions made them almost unique in American society. The typical southern planter belonged to a society that traditionally was paternalistic, not capitalistic. As a matter of fact, Genovese insists, "the planters were not mere capitalists; they were pre-capitalist, quasi-aristocratic landowners who had to adjust their economy and ways of thinking to a capitalistic world market." [16] Sutpen was a puritan, Brooks insists, who adhered to a Protestant work ethic. He worked hard merely for the sake of working, and he did so among a people who always reserved some time for leisure, despite the insistence from outsiders that they could become more prosperous if they would be more diligent. He never understood the nature of the traditional society he wished to join.

As C. Vann Woodward has observed, the southern social system was based on class consciousness and anchored in a firm awareness of social responsibility and personal honor, as well as in selfless commitment to duty and a firm belief in paternalism. Since he has a false concept of the social responsibilities of one in his position, the materially acquisitive

16 Eugene Genovese, *The Political Economy of Slavery* (New York: Vintage Books, 1967), 23.

Thomas Sutpen—to whom the image of a plantation, complete with a son to inherit and a daughter to grace his parlor at social functions, was an abstract idea—could not comprehend the southern paternalistic system. "Thomas Sutpen," as Brooks notes, "is an obsessed man, living in a private dream that has little relation to reality." [17] He is never engaged by the social system to which he has attached himself.

This "awareness of social responsibility and personal honor" is a concept totally foreign to Thomas Sutpen, as it is equally meaningless to such postmodern "heroes" as Binx Bolling and Jacob Horner, although it was fundamental to such "traditionalists" as Bayard Sartoris and Lacy Buchan. As one recalls Binx's inability to understand his great-aunt Emily's philosophy of classical stoicism, he may wish to experience Walker Percy's novel in the context of such statements as this from his foster father, William Alexander Percy: "The self-communings of the Emperor, though oft cold to clamminess, convince a man he can never be less than tight-lipped, courteous and proud, though all is pain. It is saving to rest our eyes on nobility, severe and unalloyed." [18] No more than Binx Bolling and Jacob Horner, though for an entirely different reason, can Thomas Sutpen understand what profit comes to a man just from fulfilling his social obligations and rendering a service to his fellowman.

The social system of the traditional antebellum South was not only paternalistic and plantation-centered, but, according to Genovese, "the cash nexus" never "offered a permissible basis for human relations." Finally, long experience with "human slavery and its evils and with emancipation and its shortcomings did not dispose the South very favorably toward

17 Cleanth Brooks, *William Faulkner: Toward Yoknapatawpha and Beyond* (New Haven, Conn.: Yale University Press, 1978), 297.
18 William Alexander Percy, *Lanterns on the Levee* (Baton Rouge: Louisiana State University Press, 1972), 316.

such popular American ideas as the doctrine of human per-
fectibility." [19]

3

Although he never wrote fiction and professed to know little
about it, John Crowe Ransom was one of the most influential
theoretical critics produced in America in the first half of the
twentieth century. His views of the nature of a traditional society, as expressed in such essays as "Reconstructed but Unregenerate" and "Forms and Citizens," form a philosophical
base for some of the most enduring fiction written in this century, as evidenced by *The Unvanquished, The Fathers*, and
The Optimist's Daughter. The culture which Ransom wished
to recover was one firmly based on traditional values, one
unique in America, he thought, because it was founded on
European principles. Every society passes through two stages,
he once argued, the first was what he called its "pioneering"
phase in which man's primary obligation was to find a means
of assuring his livelihood. In this developmental stage the pio-
neers examined their natural surroundings and "determined
to make whatever concessions might reasonably be expected"
to secure the material necessities of life. Almost all of their
energy, their time, and their ingenuity went to feeding, cloth-
ing, and housing themselves and their family. As soon as possible they developed the trades necessary to insure the avail-
ability of these material resources and to assist in their being
transported to the places where they were required. Thus the
early settlers of a region "arrived by painful experiment at a
thousand satisfactory recipes by which they might secure their
material necessities." Once the means of providing the economic necessities has been secured, however, he believed that
a social order should move into a second phase, because pio-

19 C. Vann Woodward, *The Burden of Southern History* (Baton Rouge: Louisiana
State University Press, 1960), pp. 19–20.

neering, despite what most Americans seem to believe, is not the normal way of life. The history of western European civilization provides many examples by which the validity of this statement can be judged. The truth is that "European opinion does not make too much of the intense practical enterprises, but is at pains to define rather narrowly the practical effort which is prerequisite to the reflective and aesthetic life." The traditional society, which is the sort that has developed in Europe, is stable "or hereditable," but in the United States, which is geared to the idea of "pioneering on principle," life is "progressive"—that is, "mobile" and "antiprovincial." The American society, which makes no special efforts to develop traditions, is forever in a state of flux, propagating change, often merely for the sake of change. These changes occur so rapidly that there is no time to form an attachment to a specific manner or style of living. Americans should follow the example of their European cousins, Ransom insists, in living "materially along the inherited line of least resistance, in order to put the surplus of energy into the free life of the mind." [20]

The nontraditional society, which is the sort usually favored in America, follows the "gospel of progress," a doctrine which runs counter to the theory that man should adapt himself to his environment and demonstrate that he is intelligent enough to secure without great effort his material necessities from the great bounties of nature. He should also conclude "a truce with nature," and live with her on "terms of mutual respect and amity." No other society has attempted to demonstrate so vehemently or violently as the American one has that "the human destiny is not to secure an honorable peace with nature, but to wage an unrelenting war on nature." [21] In this turbulent aggressive society man does not

20 John Crowe Ransom, "Reconstructed but Unregenerate," *I'll Take My Stand*, 3–5.
21 *Ibid.*, 7.

have the opportunity to allow his "loving arts, religions, and philosophies" to come spontaneously into being.

A society, Ransom insists further, should propagate and pass on these economic forms, which are developed in its "pioneering" phase and which serve the principle of utility by developing such specific objects as "plough, table, book, biscuit, machine and such processes as shepherding the flock, building, baking, making war." These practical forms are of necessity a permanent part of a functional social order, and the importance of instructing successive generations in their use is obvious. "They are," Ransom writes, "short routes to 'success,' to welfare, to the attainments of natural satisfactions and comforts." [22]

As essential as these economic forms are, however, they are not the "whole purpose of the social contract." The stable, nonaggressive, traditional society—and this is the quality of the antebellum southern social order that interested Ransom most—hands down forms of another kind. If the economic forms may be referred to as "work forms," these may be called "aesthetic or play forms." A traditional society cherishes the latter as much as the former because these aesthetic forms are the "experiences that record themselves as 'art' . . . as manners or religion." Their indispensability may not be as self-evident as the economic forms; their existence, however, in a genuinely healthy society may not be denied:

> Societies of the old order seemed better aware of the extent of their responsibilities. Along with the work-forms went the play-forms, which were elaborate in detail, and great in number, fastening upon so many of the common and otherwise practical occasions of life and making them occasions of joy and reflection, even festivals and celebrations; yet at the same time by no means a help but if anything a hindrance to direct action. The aesthetic forms are a technique of restraint, not of ef-

22 John Crowe Ransom, *The World's Body* (Baton Rouge: Louisiana State University Press, 1968), 30.

ficiency. . . . They stand between the individual and his natural object and impose a check upon his action.[23]

The deterring of man's natural impulses and the insistence that he take indirect rather than direct means of gratifying his basic desires is the most significant function of these aesthetic forms. They offer, Ransom insists, no less a service than raising man from a barbarous to a civilized state, a valuable contribution of a society in which traditional action is cherished. The cave man endured no effective checks upon his behavior. He seized by the hair of the head the woman who aroused his natural erotic desires and dragged her away to his lair, where he gratified his passion. The gentleman, however, is restrained from taking direct action. He has the "fixed code of his *gens* to remember . . . he must approach" the lady who attracts him "with ceremony and pay her a fastidious courtship." Although the original desire, which may be as strong and demanding as that of the cave man, is not abandoned, it is forced to take a "circuitous route and become a romance." The woman who arouses the desire is contemplated "under restraint," approached through the labyrinths of a fixed code of behavior, but this procedure of indirection raises the woman to the status of a specific person and to that of an aesthetic, and therefore much richer, object.[24]

One example will demonstrate, I think, exactly what Ransom means. Only human beings, because they are the only creatures who cultivate aesthetic forms, are capable of the kind of feeling that Spenser, Sidney, and others have attempted to define as human love. Like all other animals, the human being feels lust, but this basically uncomplicated passion is elevated to the much more complex emotion called love through a series of carefully regulated social conventions. In a certain kind of society there is, first of all, the coming-out

23 *Ibid.*, 31.   24 *Ibid.*

party or the debutantes' ball, the official announcement of the family that the daughter is prepared to receive serious attention from the young men of the community. These occasions are followed by an active period of courtship so that the young people of both sexes can become better acquainted. (Some dating has occurred in many instances, of course, before the coming-out party, but presumably it was not of the same intensity or seriousness as that following the ball.) Gradually the number of suitors decreases until only one is left and then comes a formal engagement, followed by another series of parties and finally the wedding, the formal reception, and the honeymoon. What this series of rigidly controlled conventions proposes to effect is to refine animal passion into human love. Man begins with a natural attraction for all women, any woman, as the male animal for the bitch; but by following the pattern of activities outlined above, this attraction, though it loses none of its intensity, becomes much richer and is directed not toward *any* woman but toward *one* woman. The wanted object becomes a concrete, individualized human being. Through this procedure, and only through it, in Ransom's opinion, do we have monogamous marriage, children, and family; and the family is the basic unit of modern society, or it has been for three hundred years.

The purpose of a commonly agreed upon code of manners in a traditional society, then, is to enable man to live at a higher level than that of the simple appetites. Ransom insists that to twentieth-century man, one who has "aged" in the pure intellectual discipline of science, religion is important for its ritual, not for its dogma. He demonstrates the importance of religious ritual to the man who in the face of death no longer has an unshaken faith in personal immortality. The traditional society, one that has retained its aesthetic as well as its economic forms, will contain a religious rite to assist the civilized, but faithless, modern who is facing one of the greatest crises of his life, the death of a loved one:

The religious society exists in order to serve the man in this crisis. Freed from his desolation by its virtue, he is not obliged now to run and throw himself upon the body in an ecstasy of grief, nor to go apart and brood upon the riddle of mortality, which may be the way of madness. His action is through the form of a pageant of grief, which is lovingly staged and attended by the religious community. His own grief expands, is lightened, no longer has to be explosive or obsessive. A sort of by-product of this formal occasion, we need not deny, is his grateful sense that his community supports him in a dreadful hour. But what interests us rather is the fact that his preoccupation with the deadness of the body is broken by his participation in the pageantry, and his bleak situation elaborated with such rich detail that it becomes massive, substantial, and sufficient.[25]

The traditional society functions, then, to assist the man with a problem that his intellect and experience cannot encompass by removing his attention from the precise event producing the overwhelming question, "enlarging the terms" of the catastrophe under consideration, and assimilating "it into the form of an ornate public ritual through which the whole mind can discharge itself."[26]

The purpose of these aesthetic forms is to humanize man, to complicate his natural functions, and make them aesthetic. The function of a traditional society, Ransom reiterates, "is to instruct its members how to transform instinctive experience into aesthetic experience." The specific occasions upon which members of a traditional society may rely on ritual, rite, ceremony, or manners are "birth, marriage, death; war, peace, the undertaking of great enterprises, famine, storm; the seasons of the year, the Sabbath, the holidays."[27]

Even dueling, properly conducted according to established, fixed rules, may be considered an aesthetic form. It attempts to eliminate, or at least to reduce, impulsive human slaughter by imposing a deterrent upon direct action. It forces a period in which aroused emotions may become assuaged, imposes upon the physical act of slaughter definite regulations, and

25 *Ibid.*, 35.   26 *Ibid.*, 43.   27 *Ibid.*, 42, 43–44.

provides the antagonists an opportunity to withdraw with honor. Wars, too, were once fought by a specific segment of the population, under carefully controlled conditions, at prescribed times (between daybreak and sunset), and often in previously agreed upon places. Occasionally the winner was determined by single combatants representing the two sides. Only when these "aesthetic" controls were lifted, as Faulkner demonstrates in *The Unvanquished*, did war result in nothing but senseless slaughter and useless destruction of personal property. Man has created a monster that even civilized behavior cannot control.

A traditional society, Ransom says, will value these aesthetic forms, which really work as a means of restraint on human behavior. They are not economic in intent or in result. "They do not butter our bread," he writes; "they delay our eating of it. They stand between the individual and his natural object and impose a check on his actions." The southern past that Ransom would attempt to reconstruct was one that placed appropriate value on these aesthetic forms—myth, rituals, manners, rites and ceremonies—one that permitted the creation and consumption of art and allowed its members to live by the credo: "In manners, aristocratic; in religion, ritualistic; in art, traditional." Much of the fiction produced in the South between the two wars reflected the attitude expressed in this credo, but these are the same kinds of belief that Binx Bolling admits he "couldn't make heads nor tails of," that they actually impede his search, his attempt to define his role in an apparently meaningless universe.

4

Alone among the southern postmoderns, Flannery O'Connor was concerned with the dogma of religion, not its ritual. We live in an age of disbelief, she wrote in *Mystery and Manners*, but the age is spiritual. For some writers, such as William Faulkner, man has within him a spirit of courage and dignity, humility and pride, that will insure his endurance, and he must not expect more. Other southern writers of the twentieth century have stated the necessity of a belief in a Supreme Being, but few, I believe, have insisted that He must be a deity who can be received sacramentally. Most moderns believe that man can neither approach his God nor be approached by Him. (Such a deity is described by Ransom in *God Without Thunder*.) Others, as Leonard Casper says of Robert Penn Warren, write with an assurance that there is a movement upward toward a superior state of being and that "present agony is meant to be rehearsal of future glory, that to avoid assimilation by matter" one "must finally accede to divine absorption." In Warren's fiction: "There is admission of a continuum of selves. Anything short of that would be mutilation, denial of cycles of dreams and seasons of memories. But the momentum of these same mechanisms for self-assurance reaches back acknowledging the past; reaches out, covering human multitudes under the beatitude of one common skin; reaches up, for assumption into the Mystical Body."[28] This description of man's relationship to metaphysical reality would clearly fall into what O'Connor calls man's belief in "The God of the philosophers."

Other twentieth-century writers, O'Connor writes, and here one could include Walker Percy, can neither believe nor be satisfied with their unbelief; therefore they search desperately for the lost God or for an entity to replace Him. Some of the most acute thinkers and writers of contemporary society are these "searchers and discoverers"; others (and one thinks of John Barth's Jacob Horner) attempt to "domesticate despair and live with it."

Unlike all of these writers, O'Connor says that her fiction is always concerned with "a relationship with a supreme being" that can only be "recognized through faith." Her contin-

28 Leonard Casper, *Robert Penn Warren: The Dark and Bloody Ground* (Seattle: University of Washington Press, 1960), 171, 170.

uing responsibility as a Christian writer, she reiterates, is to attempt to make man's encounter with God plausible and understandable. In order to make such fiction effective, the writer must first attempt to rid his reader of his "sociological bias"—the view that the most important function of fiction is to create social realism—or his "clinical bias"—that everything strange "is a case study of the abnormal." What she is trying to do is to transcend "social, cultural, and economic realism" in order to give "a sense of what exists beyond them." That which exists beyond this physical realm is the God "of Abraham, Isaac, and Jacob and not of the philosophers and scholars." This Deity is an "unlimited God and one who has revealed himself specifically. It is one who became man and rose from the dead. It is one who confounds the senses and sensibilities, one known early on as a stumbling block. . . . This God is of ultimate concern and he has a name."[29] Not only does he have a name, but he is approachable by redemption through grace. The center of meaning in human life is Jesus Christ; the center of destruction is the devil.

Like most of the other southern writers of her generation, Flannery O'Connor also writes of the collision of the past and the present, and like them, she does not believe that man's imperfections can be removed by technology and reason. She saw with alarm, as did many of her contemporaries, that the South was becoming less southern, but her standards of value are not those of the antebellum South. To find the society in which her view of man's plight and his imminent salvation was dominant, one would have to go, as Warren, Tate, and Ransom point out, backward to a time before the English Renaissance. Her concern was not, to repeat Lewis P. Simpson's terms, "the order of being in relation to existence in time," but "the order of being in relation to transcendence."[30] Al-

---

29 Flannery O'Connor, *Mystery and Manners*, ed. Sally and Robert Fitzgerald (New York: Farrar, Straus, and Giroux, 1969), 160, 161, 163, 165.
30 Simpson, *The Dispossessed Garden*, 75.

though in her fiction, place is "identified concrete, exact, and exacting," and although it functions primarily "to attach precise local values to feelings," her stories and novels are unlike those produced by any of her contemporaries. Apart from the superb individualization of her characters, an always dependable ear for the idiom of southern speech, and a hard-to-imitate knowledge of structure, her uniqueness to a large degree was the result of the subjects that she employed in her stories and her attitude toward them. She once wrote with absolute candor: "I don't think you should write something as a novel around anything that is not of the gravest concern to you and everybody else, and for me this is always the conflict between an attraction for the Holy and the disbelief in it that we breathe in with the air of the times."[31] This concern for man's belief in a personal God affected her fiction so much that her southern heritage becomes almost incidental. Place does not function in her fiction as it does in that of Welty or Faulkner.

Needless to say, her fundamental concerns are not those of most of her contemporaries. Many of the southern writers whose most important work appeared after World War II did not believe, as Lewis Simpson has pointed out, that they could restore even in the imagination "the temporal and transcendent nature of history by dramatizing in story, poem, and essay the conflict between the reality which had long supported Western civilization and the Faustian dreams of modernity."[32] Unlike Faulkner, Tate, Warren, and their European contemporaries—Eliot, Yeats, and Mann—the writers in the South after World War II—like their counterparts in the North and in Europe—Heller, Pynchon, Bellow, Camus, Sartre—become much more concerned with the very personal problem of how they can establish a meaningful relationship

31 Quoted by Lewis Lawson, "Flannery O'Connor and the Grotesque," in Robert Reiter (ed.), O'Connor (St. Louis: B. Herder, n.d.), 51.
32 Simpson, The Dispossessed Garden, 90.

with an unsympathetic universe. To them the only significant
motivation for the creation of imaginative literature was to
investigate the means by which the integrity of the individual
psyche could be preserved. Except for setting, it is difficult
to differentiate between the contemporary southern novel
and the fiction produced in New York, Chicago, or Paris. Ad-
mittedly, much contemporary southern fiction is set in the
South, but the region furnishes merely unindividualized space,
not scene in the Welty sense in which place "partakes of feeling," precise local values being attached to feeling. Walker
Percy's *The Moviegoer*, as previously pointed out, could just
as well have been set in a suburb of Rochester or Phoenix, except that some of the characters (notably Emily) express sen-
timents that were bred in an older southern culture. Even this
evidence of Southernness, in the least southern city south of
the Mason-Dixon line, is for Binx a deterrent to his search,
the central issue in the book. In John Barth's *The End of the
Road*, which is set in and around Salisbury and the Eastern
Shore, there seems to be a deliberate blurring even of the scene,
as if the author is emphasizing by this means that Jacob Horner is anyone living anywhere. Like Tate's "new provincial"
he is caught up in the present moment. His only identifying
trait is that he is contemporary man. He is alone, not associated with any tradition except that usually defined as existential.

II Pioneering on Principle: William Faulkner's The Unvanquished

The Unvanquished (1938), one of Faulkner's most underrated and least understood novels, delineates with clarity and vividness the process by which an established social order may be destroyed and, at the same time, suggests the means by which some of the values of a traditional society may be perpetuated. Writing in *The World's Body* (1938), John Crowe Ransom pointed out that "societies of the old order" handed down both "economic forms" (work forms) and "aesthetic" forms (play forms). Both kinds of forms, he insisted, are necessary for the survival of a social order. One reason that modern society is unable to satisfy the wants and demands of its members is its "horror of empty forms and ceremonies, of their invitation to men . . . to handle their objects as rudely as they can," a sure and certain means of "destroying old arts and customs" and exposing . . . their own solidarity to the anarchy of too much greed."

What Ransom is arguing, of course, is that a code of manners allows man a way of life much more rewarding than one dominated by the "stupidity of an appetitive or economic life." By extension, too, the social order that cherishes its aesthetic forms as well as its economic forms provides for a fuller life than is otherwise available. But of even greater significance is the fact that a civilization is often protected and perpetuated by its aesthetic rather than by its economic forms. Any social order reflects the imperfections of the human beings of which it is composed; therefore it contains within it the involvements, sins, disgressions, and mistakes of its selfish and greedy citizens—all those elements that would destroy it. And since there will be no perfect societies, any social order is always subject to failure. Because man cannot obliterate his own imperfections and those of the other members of the social order to which he belongs, he must always attempt to hold in abeyance the destructive elements in his society through the use of these aesthetic forms: its codes, rites, rituals, rules, and ceremonies. Only through a society that honors and cherishes these forms is man transformed into a civilized human being.

A social order fully cognizant of the significance of the aesthetic forms may have existed in the South before the Civil War, but this society fell before the ravages of the most destructive war in our history. In that conflict restrictive war—one fought among certain classes of citizens and in a relatively confined area—for the first time gave way to a total war, one that involved an entire society. With this crisis began the dissolution of all order in Yoknapatawpha County, and to the extent that Yoknapatawpha is a microcosm of the Western world, one can see—in Faulkner's delineation of how Snopeses come to dominate this fictional county in northeast Mississippi—how Western European civilization may be destroyed.

2

Convincing evidence of the process by which a traditional social order may be dissolved is revealed by a careful examination of the effects of war upon some of the characters in *The Unvanquished*. The novel opens in 1863, a most significant time because Lincoln has just issued the Emancipation Proclamation freeing the black men (and the enslavement of the black is one of the major sins committed by the leadership of the antebellum South). Too, Vicksburg and Corinth have both fallen, leaving all of north Mississippi open to assault by an invading enemy army. Colonel John Sartoris has just been voted out of command of the infantry regiment he raised and took to Virginia when the war first broke out; consequently he returns to Yoknapatawpha, raises a group of irregular cavalry (he says to protect the defenseless women and children), and sets about building pens in the swamp in order to conceal his own livestock from the enemy.

The Colonel's young son Bayard, who is only twelve in 1863, for the first two years of the war has regarded the whole enterprise as something of a lark and has spent most of his free time playing war games with Ringo, a young black of his own age. Soon, however, the nature of the game changes, for they see a troop of Yankee soldiers approaching. They carry the old family musket, one at each end as if it were a log of wood, and they reach a spot behind a honeysuckle vine just as a rider comes around the curve. They cock the musket and fire without aiming and bring down a horse. They run toward the house yelling, "We shot him, Granny. We shot the bastud." Granny, who is Rosa Millard, Colonel Sartoris's mother-in-law, looks at her grandson and asks, "Bayard Sartoris, what did you say?" And Ringo, to underscore what Bayard has already revealed exclaims, "We shot the bastud, Granny! We kilt him!"

Recovering her composure quickly because she hears a step on the porch, she says calmly, "Quick! Here!"

And then [Bayard says] Ringo and I were squatting with our knees under our chins, on either side of her against her legs . . . and her skirts spread over us like a tent . . . . We couldn't see; we just squatted in a kind of faint gray light and that smell of Granny that her clothes and bed and room all had, and Ringo's eyes looking like two plates of chocolate pudding and maybe both of us thinking how Granny had never whipped us for anything in our lives except lying.[1]

They are startled, therefore, to hear Granny say that there are no children on the place, that she has never seen the old musket the sergeant brings in. Granny is counting heavily on the fact that the colonel in charge of the troop is a gentleman, whose actions are restricted accordingly. There are certain things he will not do: he will not doubt a lady's word and even if he did, he certainly will not ask her to raise her skirt in order for him to see if anything or anybody is hidden beneath it.

Rosa Millard is forced, therefore, to violate her code of honor to protect the two boys. She is certainly aware that the colonel knows exactly where her grandson and Ringo are, but she realizes, too, that she has an advantage over the Union officer. Because of the code under which he is operating, Colonel Dick is not allowed to embarrass a lady. So Rosa violates the code for pragmatic reasons, and the error of her behavior is not rectified by her subsequent attempt to wash away the lies and improper language with harsh lye soap.

The times are so badly out of joint that Rosa Millard cannot keep the family together without violating the traditional code again. Her property has been stolen (her silver and her mules), or it has strayed away from home (her slaves), and she sets about trying to retrieve it. First, Loosh, one of the Sartoris slaves, tells a Yankee patrol where the family silver is buried, then having heard he has been freed by the proclamation of the president of the United States—or, as he expresses it—"God's own angel proclamated me free and gonter general me to Jordon"—he takes his wife Philadelphia and wanders off in search of Jordan. These events follow closely the loss of the two Sartoris mules, Old Hundred and Tinney, taken by a Yankee cavalry patrol while Rosa and the two boys are

---

1 William Faulkner, *The Unvanquished* (New York: Vintage, 1965), 32. This edition was reproduced photographically from the first edition (1938). Subsequent page references will be given in the text.

on their way to Memphis. So Rosa sets out to find Colonel Dick, the officer who has searched for Bayard and Ringo, who though a Yankee is a gentleman and will certainly return to a lady property that rightfully belongs to her. She finds Colonel Dick when he is confronted with the baffling military problem of trying to get his troops across a rain-swollen and logfilled river and then of destroying the bridge in order to escape the hordes of dazed freedmen seeking the promised land that lies across Jordan. She finds the harried colonel and explains her problem to him; he asks her to describe her stolen property. It includes, she says, a "chest of silver tied with hemp rope. The rope was new. Two darkies, Loosh and Philadelphy. The mules, Old Hundred and Tinney" (125). In the clamor and confusion of dozens of people demanding immediate solutions to insoluble problems, the colonel asks his orderly if he has a written account of the lady's request and he says he has. He has written:

> Field Headquarters
> —th Army Corps,
> Department of Tennessee
> August 14, 1863
>
> To all Brigade, Regimental and Other Commanders: You will see that bearer is repossessed in full of the following property, to wit: Ten (10) chests tied with hemp rope and containing silver. One hundred ten (110) mules captured loose near Philadelphia in Mississippi. One hundred ten (110) Negroes of both sexes belonging to and having strayed from the same locality.
>
> You will further see that bearer is supplied with necessary food and forage to expedite his passage to his destination.
>
> By order of the General Commanding. (127–28)

With the production of this document, unexpected events occur with startling rapidity. Although Uncle Buck McCaslin has warned Bayard that he is now *the* Sartoris and that he must protect Rosa and the people on the plantation in the Colonel's absence, it is Ringo, who Colonel Sartoris has repeatedly said is smarter than Bayard, who assumes the position of leadership. When Granny is reluctant to accept the additional mules, those that don't belong to her because she acquired them through the enemy's error, Ringo attempts to soothe her conscience by saying, "Hit was the paper that lied; hit wasn't us." Granny is forced into an even more absurd moral distinction: "The paper says a hundred and ten. We have a hundred and twenty-two." Even though Ringo protests, "They stole them before we did," she insists: "But we lied. . . . Kneel down." Again, she has violated a stipulation of the traditional code that gives order and direction to her life. She has taken property that does not belong to her, but, she reasons, she has not deliberately stolen it; it has come to her through accident, good fortune, or maybe by an act of Providence.

Rosa Millard's next violation of the code is even more serious than the first two aberrations were. She is not taking an unfair advantage of a gentleman in order to protect her grandson and his playmate, nor is she accepting property that fell into her hands through a stroke of good fortune. She has entered into a scheme with Ringo and Ab Snopes through which she steals horses from the enemy and sells them back to him, except those whose brands cannot be altered. Her only excuse for her actions is that she is not stealing for personal profit. The money she gets from the stolen mules she divides among her neighbors, and the mules whose brands she cannot change she distributes among her neighbors to replace the animals the enemy has stolen from them. Her reasoning is obviously pragmatic. Desirable results justify the means necessary to effect them. But, I repeat, unrestricted war has driven her to the same unscrupulous means the enemy is using in order to protect herself and her friends and neighbors from inevitable extinction. Rosa Millard's prayer indicates the degree of her contrition for the sins she has committed. She does not cringe or ask for mercy or forgiveness; her prayer, as Cleanth Brooks has pointed out, is "notably lacking in awe and reverence and humility."[2]

> I have sinned. I have stolen, I have borne false witness against my neighbor . . . and . . . I have caused three children to sin. . . . But I did not sin for gain or greed. . . . I did not sin for revenge. I defy You or anyone to say I did. I sinned first for justice. And after that first time, I sinned for more than justice; I sinned for the sake of food and clothes for Your own creatures who could not help themselves—for children who had given their fathers, for wives who had given their husbands, for old people who had given their sons to a holy cause, even though You have seen fit to make it a lost cause. What I gained, I shared with them. It is true that I kept some of it back, but I am the best judge of that because I, too, have dependents who may be orphans, too, at this moment, for all I know. And if this is sin in Your sight, I take this on my conscience, too. Amen. (167–68)

That Faulkner would have us know the seriousness of Rosa Millard's plight is further indicated by the name of the chapter in which the scheme that she has devised to strike back at the enemy is described in greatest detail. Faulkner calls this chapter "Riposte in Tertio." A "riposte," of course, is the response with which one follows up a successful thrust in fencing.[3] Caught up in a war in which all rules regulating its

---

2 Cleanth Brooks, *William Faulkner: The Yoknapatawpha Country* (New Haven, Conn.: Yale University Press, 1963), 94.

3 The "tertio" or "tierce" position in fencing is one in which the handle of the sword is grasped with the fingers pointing downward and the back of the hand upward. The position with the fingers pointing upward is usually considered more secure for beginners because it offers less temptation to "lunge with the hands below the point." There is the further risk that the experienced fencer may disarm altogether a novice opponent. The "tierce" position is not recommended, therefore, for the inexperienced fencer. Since a "riposte" may be a direct thrust in the line of the "original attack, which has been by the force of the parry," the successful riposte often depends upon the fencer responding spontaneously and unexpectedly to his opponent's parry, catching him off of his guard and unprotected. A riposte in the "tertio" position was considered dangerous for a time in both France and Italy because since the sword was held in a lateral position with the cutting edge toward the opponent, it was almost impossible to defend against. The slightest miscalculation on the part of the defender would result in a serious

activity are disregarded, Rosa Millard is in an impossible situation. Her only response to an enemy who would destroy the society to which she belongs is one that will undermine the structure of that society. The enemy has presented a thrust for which there is no acceptable response. The enemy has determined that any means necessary to win the war are justified, and Rosa Millard's position is such that her only defense against a pragmatic opponent is to become even more pragmatic then he. But in doing so she is compelled to violate and invalidate the basic code upon which the traditional society to which she belongs is based. The code of manners of a traditional society places severe limitations on the behavior of its members. If such a society is to function, its members must follow the code and its restrictions. There are definite courses of actions, as Walker Percy's Emily Cutrer explains in a memorable passage, that a gentleman won't pursue merely because he is a gentleman. "The charge is," she says, "that people belonging to any class think they're better than other people. You're damn right we're better. We're better because we do not shrink our obligations either to ourselves or to others." [4] When a gentleman doesn't act like a gentleman, when the social and moral codes of the society are violated, therefore, one no longer automatically knows what's right and what's wrong. He must rely on his own unpredictable impulses. There are no traditional values to shape and govern individual decisions; therefore the society won't function. Because she knows there are demands a gentleman won't make of a lady, Rosa Millard is able to protect Bayard and Ringo from the enemy soldiers. In order to protect them, however, she violates the code governing genteel relations. At the time this violation seems of little significance because it is developed by Faulkner

---

wound or death. See H. A. Colmore Dunn, *Fencing* (London: G. Bell and Sons, 1931), 29, 30, 33, 35, 84, 85; and Scott D. Breckinridge and Scott D. Breckinridge, Jr., *Sword Play* (New York: A. S. Barnes, 1941), 26, 63.

4 Walker Percy, *The Moviegoer* (New York: Knopf, 1961), 223.

for comic effect, but the final toll of indiscretions such as this is very serious indeed.

After a time the *modus operandi* of the scheme which Rosa and Ringo have operated so successfully against the enemy— they have retrieved 246 stolen animals—is discovered, and the plan is scotched. As a matter of fact their partner, Ab Snopes, the father of Flem, the scion of the Snopes clan, reveals to the enemy the location of the pen where the mules are kept until they can be sold back to the enemy or distributed to their new owners. Snopes compounds his duplicity by convincing Rosa, over Bayard's and Ringo's vehement objections, that she should undertake one final venture to raise a stake to be used by her son-in-law, Colonel Sartoris, in his attempts to rebuild his own plantation. A group of scalawags, who call themselves Grumby's Independents, had appeared in Yoknapatawpha as soon as the last Yankee patrol had left the county and begun to raid "smokehouses and stables, and houses where they were sure there were no men, tearing up beds and floors and walls, frightening white women and torturing Negroes to find where money or silver was hidden" (170). This band has a thoroughbred stallion and three mares, and Ab convinces Rosa that he can easily get $2,000 for the four horses. All she has to do to get them is to write out an order similar to those she has used against the Yankees, deliver it to Grumby, and demand the mares. Then, Snopes assures her, he will take over, sell the mares, keep $500 for his part, and hand her the rest to present to the Colonel when he returns. Here Rosa of course, makes a major error of judgment; she decides that if Grumby and his band are not gentlemen, they are at least "Southern men" and "would not harm a woman." For this reason, she believes, she is in no danger even if the scheme is unsuccessful. She soothes her conscience—and it is giving her noticeably less trouble as the story moves along—about taking stolen property by saying that Grumby has stolen the horses; therefore she has as much right to them as he has.

A review of the different episodes in which Rosa Millard has been concerned will reveal the gradual but certain deterioration of her moral character. She has one strength which she uses against all antagonists: she is a defenseless, weak, elderly southern lady whose actions are severely limited by the restrictive code of the society to which she belongs. She overcomes her enemy, then, by doing the unexpected, by violating the code that should govern her actions, but as I have said, her repeated and increasingly more serious violations of this code eventually destroy her. First she lies and takes advantage of her gentlemanly enemy in order to protect Bayard and Ringo. Then she goes out to recover property that belongs to her. When her property is returned to her more than tenfold because of a mistake the enemy makes, she keeps the lagniappe that has come to her and divides it among her needy neighbors. Her good fortune has such an obviously beneficial effect upon the lives of her neighbors that she enters into a kind of Robin Hood scheme—redistributing the wealth, taking from the strong to give to the weak—with Ringo and Ab Snopes. Although her actions veer more and more toward premeditated deceit and dishonesty—and they succeed because her violations of the codes of morals and manners that have always dictated her behavior become more and more flagrant—never have her motivations been for private gain. Her attempt to steal the horses from Grumby in order to provide Colonel Sartoris with the means of restoring his plantation is the first example of her committing the directly dishonest act, of her taking advantage of the code for personal gain. The deterioration of Rosa Millard is obvious and complete. Her physical destruction by Grumby is merely a function of denouément.

What Rosa Millard does not realize, in spite of her close relationships with Ab Snopes, is that all men are not gentlemen and that there is no way to summon a generalization that will cover the treatment a defenseless old lady may expect from southern white men. The very characteristics that have been her greatest asset in her dealings with gentlemen of tradition—her defenselessness, her utter dependence upon their gentility, the apparent guilelessness of her behavior—prove to be her undoing in her confrontation with Grumby. She is the competition; she, too, is in the business of stealing mules. To him destroying her is worth the effort because she is so easy to kill. When Bayard and Ringo rush into the old abandoned cotton compress where she has gone to meet Grumby, they find her dead: "[S]he looked like she had collapsed, like she had been made out of a lot of little thin dry light sticks notched together and braced with cord, and now the cord had broken and all the little sticks had collapsed in a quiet heap on the floor and somebody had spread a clean and faded calico dress over them" (175).

3

The same kind of deterioration can be traced in Drusilla Hawks and John Sartoris. After the federal troops have burned Sartoris and taken the family silver, Rosa, Bayard, and Ringo set out to try to retrieve the silver, the mules she has lost on the road, and her two slaves. As they cross northeast Mississippi and northwest Alabama, Ringo and Bayard become aware of the tragic aspects of total war. First they notice the gutted and burned houses and barns, the destroyed wagons, carriages and other personal property. Then they examine the railroad, which Ringo had wanted to see above everything else. Now the roadbed is destroyed, the crossties are burned, and the rails are wrapped around trees. At Hawkshurst, they see Bayard's cousin Drusilla, her hair "cut short . . . she was sunburned and her hands were hard and scratched like a man's that works" (103). She explains to Rosa and the boys the noise they hear—"the hurrying feet, the sound like they were singing in panting whispers, hurrying on past the gate and dying away up the road" (113). Numberless, unorganized groups of

Negroes are searching for their promised freedom, obviously confusing the "freedom" guaranteed by the Emancipation Proclamation with the only other kind of "freedom" they know: that sung of and offered in the white man's churches they have attended:

> They began to pass in the road yonder. . . . We couldn't count them; men and women carrying children who couldn't walk and carrying old men and women who should have been at home waiting to die. They were singing, walking along the road singing, not even looking to either side. The dust didn't even settle for two days, because all that night they still passed; we sat up listening to them, and the next morning every few yards along the road would be the old ones who couldn't keep up any more, sitting or lying down and even crawling along, calling to the others to help them; and the others—the young strong ones —not stopping, not even looking at them. I don't think they even heard or saw them. "Going to Jordan" . . . . "Going to cross Jordan." (103–104)

As Andrew Lytle has noted, "the uprooted slaves" are just another example of chaos replacing the order of a traditional society.[5]

Having lost her fiancé in the war, Drusilla is restless; she wants to be involved in the action and resents the only opportunities available to her in a rigidly organized social order:

> Living used to be dull, you see. Stupid. You lived in the same house your father was born in, and your father's sons and daughters had the sons and daughters of the same Negro slaves to nurse and coddle; and then you grew up and you fell in love with your acceptable young man, and in time you would marry him, in your mother's wedding gown, perhaps, and then you settled down forevermore while you got children to feed and bathe and dress until they grew up, too; and then you and your husband died quietly and were buried together maybe on a summer afternoon just before suppertime. Stupid, you see. (114–15)

The stereotype role in life to which Drusilla is objecting, her own, that which she is pleased the war has completely de-

---

5 Andrew Lytle, *The Hero with the Private Parts* (Baton Rouge: Louisiana State University Press, 1966), 121.

stroyed, is very near the station that Davidson, Ransom, and Tate would insist that woman should occupy in a traditional society.

Before the Sartorises leave for Jefferson, she requests that Bayard ask his father if she can come and ride in his troop. "Tell him," she says, "I can ride, and maybe I can learn to shoot." Although Bayard did not give his father Drusilla's message, seven months after their visit to Hawkshurst, Rosa and Bayard have a letter from Aunt Louisa, Drusilla's mother, saying that her daughter has gone she knows not where, but she fears the worst because Drusilla has deliberately "tried to unsex herself by refusing to feel any natural grief at the death in battle not only of her affianced husband but of her own father" (217). A little later, after Rosa is killed, there comes a second letter, lamenting Drusilla's unwillingness "to be the bride-widow of a lost cause"—the "highest destiny" reserved for a southern woman—when her fiancé is killed at Shiloh; instead she is a "fallen woman," conducting herself in a manner Aunt Louisa is reluctant to talk about. She has joined Colonel Sartoris' troop, "bivouacking at night surrounded by sleeping men and not even bothering to put up a tent" for the Colonel and her "except when the weather was bad" (220). Aunt Louisa insists that her daughter is lost, even though Drusilla protests "I am riding in Cousin John's troop not to find a man but to hurt Yankees" (220).

After the war Drusilla comes home with the Colonel and continues to do a man's work as the Colonel attempts to restore the plantation. (It should be noted that the Colonel turns from the traditional agrarian way of life to an industrial one, devoting now the major part of his time and energies to building a railroad.) Although Faulkner is careful to point out that the Colonel shares Bayard's pallet and Drusilla sleeps on the bed "behind the quilt where Granny used to sleep," Aunt Louisa, Mrs. Habersham, and Mrs. Compson are well aware, they think, of the ends to which a man and a woman share common quarters. They come out to find "a thin sunburned girl in a man's shirt and pants but maybe something like a tame panther or bear" (222). The good ladies insist that Drusilla must resume her role as woman by donning a dress and that convention requires that she and Colonel Sartoris marry. Drusilla tries to avoid the dress by hiding down by the spring, but the Colonel finds her and pulls her to her feet, saying, "What's a dress? . . . It don't matter. Come. Get up, soldier" (231). The ladies refuse to realize the obsolescence of their social code; they are unaware that life in the South has reverted to a much less civilized state, one in which the struggle for existence is of primal importance. They act, therefore, as if nothing has changed. They insist that the Colonel and Drusilla marry for the sake of appearances, forcing them into a loveless union, an action that frustrates Drusilla so completely that she loses whatever personal direction she has left.

The point Faulkner is making in his treatment of Drusilla is not that a woman should act as a woman but that the destructiveness of an all-out war has made it impossible for her to accept the role she would naturally occupy in a traditional society. She has not been allowed the opportunity for her courtship of the Colonel to follow the order that such an aesthetic form would assume in a traditional society; therefore human love, the basis of the institution of marriage, is likely not a part of the arrangement she and the Colonel have made. How fatally she is wounded by the war, and by the stupid treatment of the women for whom appearance is the only reality, is revealed in the last chapter of the novel. Bayard survives by altering the code to make it functional in a drastically changed society. But Drusilla is destroyed, essentially if not actually, because she has lost her faith in the code and retains only a respect for its superficial outer trappings. According to this code, one can demonstrate his courage, his right to live, only by exercising the most noble heritage he has, "to be permitted to kill, to be permitted vengeance, to take into your bare hands the fire of heaven that cast down Lucifer" (274). This is the most convincing argument urging Bayard to destroy the man who has killed his father. Only his ability to perceive clearly the circumstances under which his father died allows him to demonstrate his courage so that he can continue to occupy a position of importance in the community and maintain his self-respect without continuing the barbaric custom of useless bloodletting. As Bayard rides from Oxford to Jefferson he has a vision of Drusilla, one that leaves the reader in doubt of what this obviously disturbed young man will do until the very end of the novel:

> (I could see her, in the formal brilliant room arranged formally for obsequy, not tall, not slender as a women is but as a youth, a boy, is, motionless, in yellow, the face calm, almost bemused, the head simple and severe, the balancing sprig of verbena above each ear, the two arms bent at the elbows, the two hands shoulder high, the two identical duelling pistols lying upon, not clutched in, one to each: the Greek amphora priestess of a succinct and formal violence). (252)

4

When Sartoris is voted out of command of the infantry regiment he has organized and led in Virginia, he comes home to raise a troop of irregular cavalry. He says he has organized the troop and is acting outside the regulations of the official Confederate Army in order to give the best protection possible to the defenseless women and children of Yoknapatawpha County, now that there are enemy troops in the vicinity. But the motivation for his action may be more complex; he may be acting partially out of wounded pride because the regiment he has raised and outfitted almost single-handedly has given a vote of no confidence in his leadership, and has acted to replace him with Thomas Sutpen, the largest landowner in the county, an "underbred, a cold and ruthless man." The real significance of Sartoris's withdrawal from the organized army may be that he has removed himself from the restrictive codes under which wars were once fought. He has no authority over his actions now stronger than his own individual mind and will. He is separated from Grumby now by the only restrictions that remain on his personal behavior: those that have come to him from the traditional society that produced him.

After the war, when organized law enforcement is absent from the land, he takes the law into his own hands. He kills the two carpetbaggers who are trying to elect Cassius Q. Benbow, the former carriage driver of the Benbow family, marshal of Yoknapatawpha County. He is careful to kill these men under rules of his own devising. He has provoked them into a fight so that he appears to be defending himself. He does let them reach for their guns first, but they are no match for him, a trained gun fighter, who, like Doc Holliday of Wyatt Earp fame, has developed a trick holster so that he can draw and fire his derringer faster than the less expert gunman can begin to raise his weapon. Then he turns himself in, posts a peace bond—as Granny has before him, he makes a travesty of an important social form in a traditional society—returns to the plantation and holds a very unusual "democratic" election, in which C. Q. Benbow does not receive a single vote. His image of the significance of aesthetic forms in his society is as blurred as Granny's becomes just before her death.

Several years after the war, when he and his partner, Ben Redmond, are in the process of building the railroad, John Sartoris comes home one night, and Bayard sees him cleaning the derringer he has used to kill a "hill man, almost a neighbor." Sartoris says the man was trying to rob him, but again his father's motives are not clear to Bayard because, he says, "we were never to know if the man actually intended to rob Father or not because Father had shot too quick," and besides the dead man "had been in the first infantry regiment when it voted Father out of command" (254–55). At any rate the next day Sartoris sends some money to the dead man's wife, who lives with several children in a dirt-floor cabin. Two nights later she walks into the Sartoris house while the family is gathered around the dinner table and flings the money in Sartoris's face. The resemblance of this man to the little Colonel on the clay-bank stallion in the first of the novel is remote indeed.

As the railroad is finished, Sartoris and Redmond dissolve their partnership, Sartoris defeats Redmond for a seat in the state legislature, and then begins to taunt him deliberately with the apparent intention of killing his former friend and business partner. "He was wrong," Bayard says; "he knew he was when it was too late for him to stop." Bayard realizes the extent of his father's disintegration most dramatically, however, because of the manner in which the Colonel reacts to an event that occurs the summer before Bayard's last year at the law school of the University of Mississippi. The year is 1874 and Bayard is twenty-four. He and his stepmother are walking in the garden when she tells him to kiss her: "So I leaned my face down to her. But she didn't move, standing so, bent lightly back from me from the waist, looking at me; now it was she who said, 'No.' So I put my arms around her, Then she came to me, melted as women will and can, the arms with the wrist- and elbow-power to control horses about my shoulders, using the wrists to hold my face to hers until there was no longer need for the wrists" (262).

As soon as she releases him, Bayard's first thought is "Now I must tell Father" because he knows he does not feel like a man should after he has kissed his father's wife. He has enjoyed the erotic embrace of his stepmother, and the code demands that he report this violation to his father. So Bayard finds Colonel Sartoris in the study and faces him, standing on the rug before the cold hearth. After getting his father's attention, he tries to tell him but realizes his father is preoccupied. After dinner he does tell his father, and his father responds: "You are doing well in the law, Judge Wilkins tells me. I am pleased to hear that. I have not needed you in my affairs so far, but from now on I shall." It is then that Bayard realizes the level to which his father has sunk; it is not that the Colonel has not heard what Bayard thinks is a confession of a disgraceful act, but that he doesn't care. The change that the war has effected in John Sartoris's character is clearly revealed in two passages, one appearing near the beginning of the novel and one near the end. At the beginning of the war, Bayard admits, "He was not big, it was just the things he did that made him seem big to us." After the war George Wyatt, a member of the Colonel's irregular cavalry troop, says that Sartoris' difficulty is that he has had to kill too many men, and Bayard expresses his awareness of his father's "violent and ruthless will to dominate." In the past two years, he says, John Sartoris' eyes have "acquired that transparent film which the eyes of carnivorous animals have and from behind which they look at a world which no ruminant ever sees, perhaps dares to see, which I have seen before on the eyes of men who have killed too much" (266).

5

Bayard learns about the nature of true courage on the day he meets Redmond to make him pay for killing Colonel Sartoris. Drusilla has told him, half hysterically, how fortunate he is, how when he is an old man he can say to himself, "I have tasted all things." Then she seems to realize that Bayard is not going to fulfill her concept of justice, which to her is little more than an abstract term. "'Why, he's not—' she said. 'He's not —And I kissed his hand,' she said in a aghast whisper.'"; then she begins to laugh, "the laughter rising, becoming a scream . . . spilling between her fingers like vomit, the incredulous betrayed eyes still watching me across the hand" (275). She has to be led from the room. Aunt Jenny Dupre, the Colonel's younger sister, asks if Bayard is going to kill Redmond and Bayard says he is. "Don't kill him because of Drusilla," she responds, "a poor hysterical young woman," and don't do it because of Colonel Sartoris because he's already dead. Don't do it because of George Wyatt and the community of Jefferson. "I know," she concludes, "you are not afraid" (276). Although Bayard vows he is not going up against Redmond because of Drusilla, his father, or George Wyatt, he finds himself in a situation identical to the Grumby affair: as Uncle Buck has told him earlier, once again he is *the* Sartoris; he occupies a particular position in the eyes of Jefferson and the people of the community expect a certain quality of behavior from him.

On his way to Jefferson, then, he must refuse Ringo's offer of assistance in bushwhacking Redmond, as he does George Wyatt's to do the deed for him. He must refuse their pistols, as he has those of Drusilla and Professor Wilkins, already offered. He goes alone up the stairs, along the corridor to the door marked "B. J. Redmond," pauses for a moment, knocks, opens it, and walks in. There behind a desk, "freshly shaven and with clean linen" sits his father's former law partner, the person whom everyone, including Redmond himself, expects Bayard to try to kill. Bayard quickly surveys the room, notes the absence of whiskey or cigarette fumes and observes that Redmond's hand holds a pistol flat on the table. One is impressed with how much this scene is like that in which Colonel Sartoris has killed the two carpetbaggers. Bayard walks steadily toward the desk. No word is spoken. The pistol rises steadily from the desk. Bayard describes what he sees and hears:

> I watched it, I could see the foreshortened slant of the barrel and I knew it would miss me though his hand did not tremble. I walked toward him, toward the pistol in the rocklike hand, I heard no bullet. Maybe I didn't even hear the explosion though I remember the sudden orange bloom and smoke as they appeared against his white shirt as they had appeared against Grumby's greasy Confederate coat; I still watched that foreshortened slant of barrel which I knew was not aimed at me and saw the second orange flash and smoke and heard no bullet

that time either. . . . I looked at his face and I knew what it was to want air. (286–87)

After the second shot, Redmond rises, takes his hat from the rack, goes through the door, walks down the stairs and into the street where George Wyatt and the other members of the Colonel's cavalry troops are sitting (all of whom think Bayard has been killed). He says nothing to anyone but walks straight to the depot where the southbound train is waiting, boards it, and never comes to Jefferson again. When Bayard comes through the door, George Wyatt is perplexed. First, he asks, "You took the pistol away from him and then missed him *twice?*" Then, he answers his own question. "No; wait. You walked in here without even a pocket knife and let him miss you twice. . . . You ain't done anything to be ashamed of. I wouldn't have done it that way. . . . But that's your way or you wouldn't have done it" (288–89). Bayard has learned what courage is; it is not a mere abstraction. If it took courage for him to face Redmond unarmed, he knows it took even more, perhaps, for Redmond to pass that group of men, each of whom was certain that Redmond had killed him. Important to the point of this essay, though, is Bayard's maintaining the position the code expects *the* Sartoris to occupy and to be able to do so without perpetuating needless slaughter. Within the framework of the code, he has acted both courageously and traditionally, and, with Redmond's help, he deferred briefly the destruction of one of the bases of a traditional society.

It may be that the Civil War came, as Malcolm Cowley and others have suggested, as a kind of retributive justice for the white man's cheating the Indian out of the land and instituting the barbarous system of human slavery. But regardless of its origin, the results of the chaotic force of this total war were to undermine the foundations upon which the traditional antebellum southern society had been based. Like any other civilized society, the South had fought off the forces that would destroy it through strict adherence to a code of ethics, morals, and manners. Bayard Sartoris' action was merely a strategy to postpone the inevitable. The violence released by a completely unrestricted war was more than the aesthetic forms of that civilized society could contain. The effect of such a war was to destroy the personal integrity of the leaders of that paternalistic society, the concepts of family unity essential to any stable social order, and finally to undermine the "accepted habits and the conventions of property" upon which the entire culture of the antebellum South was built.

III *The Gaping Abyss:*
Allen Tate's The Fathers

The ending of the revised version of *The Fathers*, much less tantalizingly ambiguous and impressive than the original, makes the status of George Posey quite clear. Rather than being the antagonist of the novel, he is, J. A. Bryant, Jr., argues, almost its hero.[1] Tate says he is a romantic hero, a statement which in the context of the novel is less than completely complimentary. At least we know now that Posey lived, restored his wife to sanity, cared for his daughter, aided Lacy Buchan, the narrator of the novel and George's brother-in-law, in many unspecified ways, and died an old man. In the original version the novel ends: "I kicked the old nag in the sides and headed back into the lane that ran by the south field. I'll go back and finish it. I'll have to finish it because he could not finish it. It won't make any difference if I am killed. If I am killed it will be because I love him more than any other man."[2] Tate's revised ending is as follows: "I went back and stayed until Appomattox four years later. George could not finish it; he had important things to do that I knew nothing about. As I stood by his grave in Holyrood cemetery fifty years later

1 J. A. Bryant, Jr., "Allen Tate: The Man of Letters in the Modern World," *Sewanee Review*, LXXXVI (Summer, 1978), 282.
2 Allen Tate, *The Fathers* (Denver: Alan Swallow, 1960), 306. Subsequent references to this novel will be to *The Fathers and Other Fiction* (rev. ed.; Baton Rouge: Louisiana State University Press, 1977). Page numbers will be given in the text.

I remembered how he restored his wife and small daughter and what he did for me. What he became in himself I shall never forget. Because of this I venerate his memory more than the memory of any other man" (306–307).One is left to puzzle out how Lacy can love a man who has killed his brother and driven his sister mad.

The essential action of *The Fathers*, as Arthur Mizener has pointed out, "is the terrible conflict between two fundamental and irreconcilable modes of existence." Perhaps the two modes are, as Bryant suggests, irreconcilable "only as parts of any paradox are irreconcilable" and that "together they constitute a paradox that characterizes all societies, American as well as those from which American societies sprang, and will undoubtedly characterize the new societies into which America must dissolve long after our present political system has vanished from the earth."[3] Bryant is arguing, then, that all societies that have existed or will exist have contained or will contain both romantic and classical elements, and these contrasting views have and will conflict. As true as that statement undoubtedly is, the critic does not recognize sufficiently the unique nature of the antebellum southern social order, when compared to the America that Matthew Arnold found so mundane and uninteresting in the 1880s. Unlike the civilization that developed in other sections of the country, that which evolved in the pre-Civil War South was a society that emphasized, as none other in America has, the importance of controlling natural, direct, impulsive action (restrictions which the romantic view would not tolerate) through the use of custom, manners, ritual, and ceremony (controls which the classical view would encourage).[4]

---

3 Bryant, "Allen Tate," 275.
4 Tate said that his primary motive for revising the ending of *The Fathers* was to give the novel two heroes: "Major Buchan, the classical hero, whose hubris destroys him; George Posey, who may have seemed to some readers a villain, is now clearly a modern romantic hero (*The Fathers*, revised edition, xxi). This

Tate has described a traditional society as one in which the "presiding spirit" is that the "way of life and the livelihood of man must be the same" and the "way we make our living must strongly affect our way of life." The traditional man is one not only "surrounded by the grandeurs of the past" but one who is able "to participate in them." In a very genuine sense he is sustained by them. Because he is able to exercise his intellect for a predetermined purpose—to sustain the principles upon which human existence at its most nearly complete level is based—it is an instrument which he can control and properly use.[5] The nontraditional man (or the romantic) has no confirmed belief in the "manners, morals, or codes" supported by a well-established social order that honors both its aesthetic and its economic forms; therefore his "indestructible vitality demands expression in violence and chaos." He has lost both the "higher myth of religion and the lower myth of history" as means of controlling his decisions and actions. He must capitulate, then, to his subhuman role, to a "series of pragmatic conquests." In this novel we have the perfect contrast between the traditional man who attempts to maintain the "historical myth" of how man must conduct himself in the face of life's inevitable crises, and the nontraditional man who relies upon no means of controlling his personal actions except his own impulses. Tate has written that although man has never achieved "a perfect unity between his moral nature and his economics," he has never failed so dismally as he has now."

Antebellum man, insofar as he achieved a unity between his moral nature and his livelihood, was a traditional man. He dominated the means of life; he was not dominated by it. I think that the distinguishing feature of a traditional society is simply that. In order to make a liveli-

---

statement suggests, too, that Tate definitely intended the kind of conflict I am developing here.
5 Allen Tate, *Essays of Four Decades* (New York: William Morrow, 1968), 555.

hood men do not have to put aside their moral natures. Traditional men are never quite making their living, and they never quite cease to make it. . . . The whole economic basis of life is closely bound up with moral behavior, and it is possible to behave morally all the time.[6]

George Posey is the prototypical modern nontraditional man who is dominated by the means of life. Upon a purely rational decision, one that surely never reached his heart, for example, he sells his black half-brother to raise the funds to meet a temporary financial crisis.

I

In an introduction to *Sanctuary*, Tate remarks that before 1920 southerners wrote not a "literature of introspection" but one of "romantic illusion."[7] The antebellum literary mode, he writes in "A Southern Mode of the Imagination," was rhetorical, presupposing always a silent listener who was never expected to respond. The rival mode of the imagination, and the one responsible for much of the best writing between 1920 and 1950, he called the "dialectical," which presupposes "the give and take of two minds, even if one mind, like the mind of Socrates, prevails at the end."[8] The change in the kind of literature written in the South after 1920 was the result of the southern writers reentering the world but glancing backward as they "stepped over the border." This backward glance, the ability "to see the past in the present," successfully innoculated the southern writer of the time against the disease that struck some of his contemporaries in other sections of the country. Rather than driving him to Greenwich Village, or to the Left Bank, in search of amenable companions, acceptable patterns of behavior, and viable artistic and moral standards, the south-

6 *Ibid.*, 556.
7 Allen Tate, "Faulkner's *Sanctuary* and the Southern Myth," *Virginia Quarterly Review*, XLIV (Summer, 1968), 420. This essay appears as the introduction to the Signet edition of *Sanctuary* (1968).
8 Tate, *Essays of Four Decades*, 583.

ern writer's "double focus" encouraged him to see "an image of a recovery—a restoration, perhaps a reconstruction—of memory and history."[9] Many of the qualities the modern southern writer found missing in moral life were once an integral part of the society of his own region. Unlike his northern contemporaries, he was not "locked in the present" and forced "to live by chance."

The writers of Tate's generation, then, were able to engage in an "exercise of myth making . . . within the restricted realm of historical event." They could see the character of a historical hero, if not that of a religious one. They created a southern myth, which informed the sensibility and thought, at various conscious levels of the defeated South.[10] This myth is contained in Faulkner's greatest novels, as it is with significant variations in Tate's *The Fathers*, and it fostered much of the great writing in the South between the two wars. Tate describes this myth in general terms as follows:

> The South, afflicted with the curse of slavery—a curse, like that of Original Sin, for which no single person is responsible—had to be destroyed, the good along with the evil. The old order had a great deal of good, one of the "goods" being a result of the evil; for slavery itself entailed a certain moral responsibility which the capitalist employer in free societies did not need to exercise if it was not his will to do so. This old order, in which the good could not be salvaged from the bad, was replaced by a new order which was in many ways worse than the old. The Negro, legally free, was not prepared for freedom; nobody was trying to prepare him. The carpetbaggers, "foreign" exploiters and their collaborators, the native rascals called "scalawags," gave the Old South its final agonies. The cynical materialism of the new order brought to the South the American standard of living, but it also brought a society similar to that which Matthew Arnold saw in the North in the Eighties and called vigorous and uninteresting.
>
> The evil of slavery was twofold, for the "peculiar institution" not only used human beings for a purpose for which God had not intended

---

9 Lewis P. Simpson, *The Dispossessed Garden* (Athens: University of Georgia Press, 1975), 70.
10 Tate, "Faulkner's *Sanctuary*," 425.

> them; it made possible for the white man to misuse and exploit nature herself for his own power and glory.

This southern myth, Tate concludes, did not merely decline gradually, die of its own inertia, as Hawthorne suggests its counterpart in New England did; it was destroyed "by a great action in which the entire society was involved . . . by outsiders in a Trojan War." [11]

This myth, although it will surely appear inadequate to most outsiders, has allowed many modern southern writers, Tate among them, to dramatize much of southern historical reality. A recurring theme in Tate's poetry is the attempt to see the "past that lies behind that personal past." In "Message from Abroad," written in Paris in 1929 while Tate was on a Guggenheim grant, and dedicated to Andrew Lytle, the poet ponders the means, the process through which a culture is maintained, how tradition is passed from one generation to the next. Some cultures, the speaker in the poem points out, "Provence / The Renaissance, the Age of Pericles," are clearly preserved. Others pass into oblivion and are lost because they have no poetry. From his vantage point in Europe Tate has difficulty seeing "bony and sharp and very red" faces of his ancestors. In "Ode to the Confederate Dead," the man at the gate of the Confederate cemetery cannot make himself see charging soldiers in the falling leaves; thus the protagonist of this poem fears he is losing his awareness of the tradition out of which he comes. In a poem he wrote a few years later, "The Mediterranean," Tate was able to move out of "time's monotone," to reverse the process of Western expansion and recover his ancestral home, his spiritual roots, and he made this discovery through the use of myth and great art. This search for a meaningful relationship between his present circumstances and the traditions to which he belonged continued to dominate Tate's writings in the 1930s.

11 *Ibid.*, 426.

It is easy, and quite proper I believe, to see that the notion of a traditional society, one which can allow the existence of men who can "achieve a unity" between their moral nature and the means by which they earn their living, is very similar to the myth encompassing the society that existed in the South before the Civil War. The destruction of such a society, as Tate emphasizes and Faulkner's *The Unvanquished* demonstrates, is accomplished both from within and by a single, catastrophic action, "by outsiders in a Trojan War." Since any social order includes the imperfections of the fallible men who developed it, the society may exist only so long as it can contain "by rules and orders, accepted habits and the conventions of property," the destructive aspects of man's inheritance which would destroy it.

As I read *The Fathers*, however, Tate's most extensive treatment of this traditional society, it does not appear that his interpretation of this southern myth is quite the same as his explanation of this myth in Faulkner. *The Fathers* will support, it seems to me, the suggestion that the antebellum society had within it the elements that would have destroyed it even if the Civil War had never occurred. Tate's essay in *I'll Take My Stand* argues that the pre–Civil War South did not have the proper form of religion to support the kind of civilization it was developing. Its Protestantism was suited for a mercantile and technological order, but it would not support the section's traditional agrarian culture. He has argued, too, that the enslaved black man did not form an appropriate peasantry for an agrarian society. The reason the South developed a feudal society but not a feudal religion is not difficult to understand:

> It is just possible to see the Jamestown project as the symbol of what later happened to this country: it was a capitalistic enterprise undertaken by Europeans who were already convinced adherents of large-scale exploitation of nature, not to support a stable religious order, but to advance the interests of trade as an end in itself. They stood thus for

a certain stage in the disintegration of the European religion, and their descendants stuck to their guns, which theoretically at least were Protestant, aggressive, and materialistic guns.[12]

There was also the view that soil and climate made agrarianism more attractive as a means of securing economic goods than a less fertile soil, a colder climate, and a shorter growing season would have done. The need of an adequate and available labor supply was obvious; therefore slavery was introduced. The slave, however, was a possession of his owner, real property as the land was, and he did not in the feudal sense, as the serf did, belong to the land. The southern religion was forced to defend slavery; its religious impulse therefore was inarticulate because it was a "non-agrarian and trading religion; hardly a religion at all, but a result of a secular ambition." [13]

3

The opening scene of *The Fathers* presents vividly and clearly the "terrible conflict between two fundamental and irreconcilable modes of existence" which will destroy the antebellum southern civilization. This conflict is revealed in the "tension between the public and private life," Arthur Mizener believes, between "the order of civilization . . . imposed by discipline, and . . . the disorder of the private life . . . imposed by circumstances, and at the mercy of its own impulses." [14] As the novel opens the relatives of Major Lewis Buchan, staunch representative of the antebellum southern society, are gathered for a ceremonious occasion at his family estate, Pleasant Hill, a microcosm of that social order. Major Buchan's wife has died and the Buchan clan and their friends have gathered to

---

12 Allen Tate, "Remarks on the Southern Religion," *I'll Take My Stand* (Baton Rouge: Louisiana State University Press, 1977), 166–67.
13 *Ibid.*, 167–68.
14 Radcliffe Squires (ed.), *"The Fathers"* in *Allen Tate and His Work* (Minneapolis: University of Minnesota Press, 1972), 123.

share his grief with him. The social order at Pleasant Hill is rigidly structured by the code of manners on which it is based and clearly dependent upon the system of slavery for its perpetuation. To serve its members in crises such as that presented by Mrs. Buchan's death, the social order has a "pageantry of grief which is lovingly staged" so that the bereaved does not have "to run and throw himself upon the body in an ecstasy of grief or go apart and brood upon the riddle of mortality." His grief, therefore, is permitted to expand; it is no longer explosive or obsessive; his "preoccupation with the deadness of the body is broken by his participation in the pageantry." [15] Major Buchan moves with composure among his many guests, seeking to make them comfortable and accepting their expressions of sympathy. His own genuine grief for the wife whom he loved dearly is merged with and controlled by the other emotions aroused by this ritualistic occasion.

Among the Major's guests is George Posey, the husband of Lucy, the Major's only daughter. George, whose family has long since given up the land and moved into Georgetown, represents the "disorders of the private life," always at the "mercy of its own impulses," as opposed to the stability and order imposed by the discipline and restraints of the codes, ceremonies, and rituals of a traditional public life. The conflict is once again an epic one between romantic impulse and classical restraint. For the Poseys all semblances of family ties have disappeared. The members of the family never have a meal together. Uncle Jarman once wanted to be a man of letters, but no one else agreed with his choice of profession, so, like Poe's Roderick Usher, he becomes an overrefined recluse, viewing life as it appears to him from his dormer window and coming downstairs only once a year. He "had had so long an assured living," Tate points out, "that he no longer knew that it had a natural source in human activity" (178). George's

15 John Crowe Ransom, *The World's Body* (Baton Rouge: Louisiana State University Press, 1968), 35.

mother is "a gentlewoman who became in the common sense more and more 'gentle' as she got older, and ended up by not being able to entertain longer than a minute any thought that did not concern her health and feelings" (178). George's aunt Milly never eats anything except overripe bananas, and sniffs whenever such concrete subjects as money, childbirth or poverty are brought into the conversation. Like her sister, she never believes that common people are real, for "'it is just too painful that they should exist'" (184).

The Poseys are a family who communicate only through their infirmities, and, as its head, George Posey may be contrasted at every point with his father-in-law, Major Buchan. As Tate's romantic hero, George Posey is "without people or place," a traditionless man, one who construes the world's actions as intended for his private reaction and consumption. He is, according to Lacy Buchan from his vantage point fifty years later, "a man who received the shock of the world at the end of his nerves" (185). Because he is unable to objectify his feelings, all action becomes intensely personal to him; thus he is terribly embarrassed when he sees a little bull struggling valiantly to perform his proper function on the Buchan plantation. (Major Buchan casually remarks that the little animal is "a little young, but I reckon he's equal to the occasion"; even the refined and proper Mrs. Buchan can explain to some young girls that the bull is "here on business.") At his mother-in-law's funeral George is not a part of the community. He cannot participate in the religious pageantry; therefore he is preoccupied with the putrefying corpse, brooding "upon the riddle of mortality." Aware of the manners, rituals and rites the traditional society provides for man's support in such crises, Lacy conjectures that George "needed intensely to leave" before Mrs. Buchan's funeral, because he felt a deep compulsion "to escape from the forms of death which were, to us, only the completion of life, and in which there could be nothing personal, but in which what we were deep inside found a sufficient expression" (22–23). To George Posey death is only personal. Unaware of the rituals that traditional society provides for its members to control its destructive imperfections, George Posey does not know that life is "eternally balanced upon a pedestal" below which lies an abyss. Man can avoid the magnetic attractions of the abyss only by strict adherence to the restrictive code of the traditional society. Unlike George Posey, Major Buchan knows so well the code forming the social order to which he belongs that his actions automatically avoid its prohibitions. Life to him is an intricate game with a definite set of rules which he expects everyone to know and follow. He is not prepared, therefore, to deal with a man like George Posey who allows no restraints upon the course of action suggested by his deepest impulses.

4

As Lacy remembers his mother's funeral and George's unusual behavior on that occasion, he recalls other incidents that allow the reader to fix Posey's position in relation to the traditional society of Pleasant Hill. Once, Lacy remembers, George surprised him with the gift of an expensive shotgun. When Major Buchan protests that his family has done nothing to deserve such kindness—George is merely an acquaintance of Lacy's brother Semmes—George explains his generosity by saying he acted on impulse: "'Major Buchan,' he said, 'I have expressed only my feelings of respect for your family, sir. I have said nothing about kindness. If you refer to the gun, why, the boy would have had one sooner or later. . . . I didn't buy it for him. I took pleasure in just buying it; . . . I was coming here and I thought I'd just give it to Lacy'" (35).

The conflict between George Posey and Major Buchan, and the basic attitudes that motivate it, is never more apparent than in the episode in which George asks the Major for Susan's hand in marriage, a custom that George considers utter nonsense. The Major, for his part, is convinced that

George, not being a gentleman, does not know how to conduct himself on such an important occasion. Lacy is sitting on an ottoman in his father's study, glancing through a copy of *Ivanhoe* and thinking of the tournament to be held the following Saturday in Fairfax, when George Posey enters. He feels immediately the tension in the air when Major Buchan fails to inquire about George's family, for Lacy understands the intricate rules under which Major Buchan conducts social intercourse:

> I knew that papa was telling George Posey in a roundabout way, the way he always told unpleasant things, that young men from distant places, like Georgetown, twenty-five miles away, who happened to become acquainted with one of his sons, had no claim upon any other member of his family. . . . I looked at papa. If, a few minutes before, the addition of his hat had framed his moustache in such a way as to make him resemble a benevolent tiger, he now . . . looked like a tiger without the benevolence.
>
> . . . .
> I winced a little: what papa had said to him would have blasted off the earth most of the people I knew, yet George Posey was affected not at all, and sat imperturbable at what I felt now was the end of the storm. Papa just looked bewildered. He could do no more—he had fired his heaviest charge short of insulting his son's invited guest. (34–35)

Later, Lacy realizes that George's ignorance of the game Major Buchan is playing is so great that he did not recognize the Major's rudeness at all; instead he thought the Major was being courteous. The Major is, in turn, flabbergasted; he has never run into a young man like this one before, one who "simply refused" to recognize the "danger signals he was sending out."

Almost immediately following this unforgivable breach of decorum, George Posey again shows his utter disregard for the ritualistic behavior of the traditional society in whose most cherished ceremonies he has become engaged. Wearing the colors of his bride-to-be, Susan Buchan, George enters the annual tournament, wins for her the grand prize, and then turns the whole affair into a ludicrous parody of the ceremonious occasion it is supposed to be. First, he outrides the perennial winner of the contest, John Langton—a "sportsman who . . . had never read a book and could hardly write a letter . . . a bold and insolent man who deemed himself an aristocrat beyond any consideration for other people" (62). When Langton steps in front of Posey as he is going to the platform to receive his prize, George "reached around Langton's neck and grabbed his shirt-front. He jerked him to him, stooped, and with that one arm raised him off the ground. Then as if he were pitching a sack of meal, he tossed him away into a heap" (68). After this display, George walks unhurriedly to the platform to receive the wreath that will proclaim Susan the "Queen of Love and Beauty." He receives the wreath and it seems as if he is going to follow the custom of placing it on her head, when suddenly he pauses, drops the wreath in her lap, draws himself up to his full height, embarrasses the crowd and humiliates Susan by laughing loudly. George is clearly expressing his contempt for what to him is useless ceremony.

Because George has humiliated him in public, the only recourse John Langton has is to challenge him to a duel, which he promptly does. George accepts and the group of men go down to the far end of the pavilion. The dueling pistols are produced and George demonstrates his skill with the weapon by hitting, almost without aiming, a small smudge he has placed on his hat. Since the distance from which he is shooting is exactly that from which the two antagonists would be facing each other, George is obviously demonstrating that he could more than hold his own if the duel were to occur. But, again, he will not participate in a senseless exercise. He flings his pistol away and hits John Langton one blow on the chin. "Langton fell back," Lacy says, "and as he rolled over on his face I saw that it was covered with blood" (75). Jim Mason speaks for his community when he expresses his attitude at George's disrespect for the ceremonious behavior that gives order to his society. "Mr. Posey," he says, "I did not in the least approve of Langton's rudeness to you, and it was equally insulting to the judges. . . . I never did like Langton, from the time we were boys. But that ain't the point. . . . You agreed to come out here and there was only one thing to come for. Not for this" (75–76).

Two other incidents, reported briefly, should suffice to demonstrate that George Posey's impulsive actions sometimes produce happy results but more often than not they lead to tragedy. I have already referred to his selling his black half-brother, Jim, because he needed $1,500. Later Jim returns to his family home and finds Jane, whom he has reared and who is not aware of their true relationship, afraid of him. He enters her room, and the sight of him there, in those surroundings, frightens her so badly she cries out and then faints. Susan comes in to answer Jane's call, finds her unconscious, and declares that Jim has tried to rape her. In order to prevent a marriage between Jane and Semmes, Susan has Jane taken to a convent and Jim "carried up the river." Here Semmes, in too frenzied and literal application of the code, shoots Jim, and George kills his brother-in-law. As Tate points out in his "Note" to the Revised Edition: "George shot Semmes not in rational revenge but in instantaneous reflex action, an instinctive response to the murder of his half-brother. It is almost as if Semmes had tried to shoot him, George himself" (313). In a vision Lacy tried to have his grandfather justify George's actions: "It was not the *intention* of your brother-in-law to kill your brother. . . . He does evil because he has not the will to do good. The only expectancy that he shares with humanity is the pursuing grave" (267; emphasis mine). Without the support of a sustaining tradition, George is entirely alone, a victim of his own impulses. He suffers "the shock of communion with a world he could not recover." The slightest unpleasant action is received as a shock at the end of his nerves.

As one would expect from a person either acting always

on impulse or choosing what seems to be the more rational course of action from the data of the moment, many of George Posey's actions are both good and evil. He saves Pleasant Hill from bankruptcy by selling the excess slaves, an act which Major Buchan will not do. Although he declares his sympathy for the federal cause, he delivers weapons, ammunition, and supplies to the Confederates—for the sole purpose, as he says, of making money. Then, he shoots John Langton, now a Confederate officer, for insulting him; even then, however, he violates the code because he gives Langton no chance to defend himself. He acts impulsively, as this time he must, because circumstance will not permit a regularized duel.

5

The Fathers suggests, then, that contrary to Cowley's view of Faulkner's southern myth, the imperfections that will destroy the antebellum southern society are unalterably at work even before the Civil War begins. This force is represented by the inevitable clash between the Buchans and the Poseys. The southern society has become so static that all personal feelings are automatically channeled through custom and ritual; therefore an individual has no existence apart from the family or the society to which he belongs. Major Buchan's refusal to recognize the fact that disunion is possible, not to say inevitable, forces his two older sons to join the Confederate army against their father's wishes, and the Major's inability to face concrete facts—much like that of the Posey women—allows Lacy to see his father in a true light:

> That was the first time, I suppose, that papa had seemed to me to speak from a great distance, as if he were a man preoccupied with some private mystery that could not be connected with what was going on in the world. . . . Where in his mind were the vast hordes of young men who were rushing to village and county town, from the river bottoms and the hills, coming with squirrel rifles, shot-guns, bowie knives, to "form military companies" in Georgia, Alabama, Mississippi, by the

banks of the James, the Chattahoochee, the Tennessee? For papa, these young men did not exist; all that country from below the James to the Rio Grande was a map, and the "war" was about to be fought between the "government" and the sons of his neighbors and kin in the old Northern Neck of Virginia. (155)

At another level Tate presents the contrast between the private and the public domains in his views of the two ministers who preside at the funeral of Lacy's mother. Mr. McBean, the Presbyterian minister, who is obviously moved by the death of a loyal member of his congregation, reacts personally and spontaneously as he moves among the mourners or says his amens at the funeral service. But, Lacy wonders, why does Dr. Cartwright, the Episcopal rector, to whose flock Major Buchan belongs, talk differently from Mr. McBean: "His words were different, he seemed to be just a voice, in the *ore rotundo* of impersonality, no feeling but in the words themselves." (105).

Like the Reverend Dr. Cartwright, Major Buchan embodies perfectly the tradition to which he belongs. If he has any personal warmth and feeling for his son Lacy, he conceals it behind the impervious mask of his formal manner. The relationship between father and son is impersonal and ceremonious. The same ritual is enacted at the beginning of each day: "As I came in [Lacy says] he laid the box on the small table by his chair, rose to his feet, and as I stood before him he leaned over and kissed me on the forehead. Then he shook hands as he said: 'God bless you, my son, in your labors of this day.' 'God bless you, Papa,' I said" (126). All their days, the reader is told, begin in this way, almost as if the manner in which father will meet son each morning is set forth as a service in *The Book of Common Prayer*.

Tate's myth of the antebellum southern civilization, then, varies somewhat from that which he suggests Faulkner and other southerners wrote. This society was not destroyed by the Civil War, as a kind of retributive justice for the white man's cheating the Indian out of the land and instituting the barbarous system of human slavery. In Major Buchan we can see that the society had already become so nearly ossified that its rituals expressed all the feelings of which the individual was capable. The person who reacts against the discipline of this formal society—that is George Posey, the romantic hero —destroys the fundamentals of its civilizing influences and is left naked and alone. Somewhere between these two extremes, then George Posey's position and that of Major Buchan, is the appropriate place for a vital and healthy social order. And it is this order which Bayard Sartoris seeks, as Lacy Buchan for fifty years views its absence from the world he inhabits.

IV The Awful Responsibility of Time: Robert Penn Warren's All the King's Men

All the King's Men is not only the best political novel in American literature, but it is one of the most profound fictive studies of modernism. As the action opens for its protagonist, Jack Burden, the past is no longer the nourishing tradition it is for Bayard Sartoris, but as the novel unfolds he gets a clearer view of his traditional past. He moves from idealism, in which he attempts to rationalize away any unpleasant facts he does not wish to accept, through a period of pragmatism, when he tries to explain every aspect of the world and the people who live in it in terms of function, until finally he reaches a view of the world as idea *and* mechanism, one which includes a metaphysic that can accommodate evil. In this philosophic quest his view of the past undergoes many changes: once seen as a terrifying skeleton that must be avoided whenever possible, the past is finally found to form, fertilize, and develop both present and future. His mature view is one in which the past cannot be approached either cynically or sentimentally but one that must be accepted realistically, with the realization that "we can keep the past only by having the future for they are forever tied together . . . only out of the past can we make a future." This is the only way man can keep his belief, and, as Robert B. Heilman has pointed out, the "fruitful deed" can only come out of "the long wisdom" that accrues from facing history and entering "that awful responsibility of time." [1] Jack Burden must find some sense of identity to fill the void in his being, what Warren in "The Ballad of Billie Potts" refers to as that part of him he has left behind as the "cicada had left at the cross roads or square, / The old shell of self, thin, ghostly, translucent, light as air." Such are the primary concerns of one of the most widely read and best known novels in modern American literature, one that has already gone through more than fifty large printings and from which a prize-winning motion picture was made.

Like many other moderns, Jack Burden feels that he can do his job and not become personally involved in the drama of life unfolding before his eyes, but, as he says, two pieces of historical research have taught him the error of this kind of thinking. At a climactic moment he became convinced that man could be "born again," but such a phenomenon could only occur if he could discover his past, if he could really know it and be fully aware of his place in it. Jack Burden had been born into what Warren once called "the world of good families," who were wealthy but not rich, but whose influence stretched backward to the founding of the state. Although his family and friends had always owned land, lots of it, and had been involved in robbing it of its long-leaf pine timber, they had served the professions of law and medicine as lucrative avocations, their primary vocations being to live as Burdens, Stantons, or Irwins, and to provide their society richly with Ransom's "aesthetic forms": manners, customs, rituals, rites and ceremonies—the civilizing aspects of a social order. Occasionally one of them would give up his financially rewarding practice of corporation law to accept an appointment as

---

1 Robert B. Heilman, "Melpomene as Wallflower; or, The Reading of Tragedy," in John Lewis Longley, Jr. (ed.), *Robert Penn Warren: A Collection of Critical Essays* (New York: New York University Press, 1965), 94.

judge or attorney general and very rarely one would accept the challenge of campaigning for and serving in the highest office in the state, that of governor. As a general rule, however, they were willing to manipulate the affairs of government from the seclusion of their libraries or law offices.

Into such a society, one very much like that described in William Alexander Percy's *Lanterns on the Levee*, was Jack Burden born, and here in Burden's Landing he lived as child, youth, and young man. His earliest memories were of a "stocky man with a black coat and spectacles" who entered the room where Jack was coloring pictures before the fire and allowed him to have a bite of candy before supper. Later on that evening, and others like it, he was carried upstairs to bed by the "woman with the pale hair and the blue eyes and the famished cheeks who leaned over me and kissed me good night and left the sweet smell in the dark after the light was out." (This woman, about whom Jack could never untangle his ambiguous feelings, was his mother.) There was also Judge Irwin; in his youth Jack thought of him as a friend of the family, who taught him to hunt, saying often: "You ought to have led that duck more, Jack. You got to lead a duck, son."[2] As Jack grew older, his mother had an assortment of husbands. When Jack was six, the Scholarly Attorney walked out; then there were others. First there was the Tycoon, then one day Jack came home to find another man, Count Covelli. After a while the Count left, to be followed by the Young Executive. Though there was a succession of husbands for Jack's mother, there was no father for Jack. The men who shared his mother's life, and attempted to satisfy her needs, were not concrete individualized human beings for Jack: they were abstractions about whom he had less feeling than he did about the furniture his mother was disposing of and acquiring almost as rap-

2 Robert Penn Warren, *All the King's Men* (New York: Harcourt Brace, 1946), 288. All references to the novel are to this edition, and page numbers are given in the text.

idly as she changed husbands. Obviously the institution of family, a fundamental of the traditional society delineated by Faulkner and Tate, has disappeared from the house where Jack Burden lives. As a grown man Jack scrutinizes the living room of the house he had grown up in:

> Well, the room had come a long way from the way I first remembered it, moving toward some ideal perfection which was in my mother's head or in the head of a dealer in New Orleans, or New York, or London, and maybe just before she died, the room would achieve its ideal perfection, and she would sit in it, a trim old lady, with piled-up hair, and silky skin sagging off a fine jawbone and blue eyes blinking rapidly, and would take a cup of tea to celebrate the ideal. (121)

Although Jack's wisecracking manner makes him seem detached from what he is observing, the reader is aware that he is deeply and profoundly affected. Apparently, his mother is employing the same set of values, fed by the same unfulfilled desires, in her search for the ideal furnishing for her house that she is using in attempting to find an appropriate mate. The flippant tone of Jack's language only makes his disgust for his mother more evident.

At any time he reminisces about his life in Burden's Landing, Jack's memory is filled with images of Anne Stanton: a little girl touching the surf with one toe on the first day of spring, or a slightly older girl with a smudge of soot on her nose as she, her brother Adam, and Jack roast weiners in the Stanton backyard. Then one day during the summer before he is going to enroll in the state university (his mother wants him to attend Princeton or Williams), he becomes aware of her as a person—as an attractive and desirable young girl— and not merely as his friend's kid sister. The image he carries around with him always is of Anne's "face lying in the water, very smooth, with the eyes closed, under the dark-greenish-purple sky, with the white gull passing over" (126). During his next four years at State, this image remained, "growing brighter as the veils were withdrawn and making the promise of a greater brightness." Although this image never left him, his attitude toward Anne changed. The summer after his graduation he and Adam continue to play tennis or swim, with Anne always tagging along. Then one evening he and Anne go to a movie alone and coming home they park along the beach and Jack has another image indelibly etched in his memory:

> Anne's face lying back, with the eyes closed and the moonlight pouring over it, and I remembered that day of the picnic long back—the day when we had swum out in the bay, under the storm clouds, when she had floated on the water, her face turned up to the purple-green darkening sky, her eyes closed, and the white gull passing over, very high. I hadn't thought of that since it happened, I guess, or if I had thought of it, it hadn't meant a thing, but all at once . . . I had the feeling of being on the teetering verge of a most tremendous discovery. (293)

Later that night, lying in his bed, Jack realizes he is in love. From that moment onward this summer becomes a kind of touchstone; he always feels that he can determine the genuineness or intensity of an emotion by comparing it to how he felt that summer. Years later Jack realizes that if things had been allowed to develop "more in the normal manner" his life might have taken a different direction. The situation he is referring to is the evening that Anne offers herself to him and all he feels is "great warm pity." At the same time he realizes "that when a half-clothed and healthy young man kneels beside a bed and seizes the hand of an entirely unclothed and good looking young girl," his reaction should not be that of feeling sorrow for her. When he understands that he has taken from her her basic humanity and reduced her to an abstraction, when he realizes that he is not in love with a woman but attracted by an ideal, the image of a young face in the moonlight, the moment for action has passed.

Though he continues to see Anne, things are never the same between them again. That summer with its magic—his life will reach fewer high peaks—passes. Jack goes to the university, while Anne attends finishing school in the East and steadfastly refuses to marry him, because his life is not centered; it has no aim or purpose. He tries to complete law school to convince her that he does have a definite objective, but the routine is so deadly that he adopts a course of action that inevitably results in his expulsion. Then, spending as little time at home as he can and even refusing his mother's offer of financial assistance, he drifts into graduate school and begins to work for a Ph.D. degree in history. To fulfill his thesis requirement, he undertakes to edit the journal of a maternal ancestor, Cass Mastern, who was killed in the Civil War. When he has accumulated all the evidence he can collect about Cass Mastern, he suddenly realizes he cannot complete the project because he does not understand Cass Mastern. While a student at Transylvania College, Cass seduced, or was seduced by, Annabelle Trice, the wife of his good friend Duncan. When Annabelle's husband discovered his friend's duplicity and his wife's unfaithfulness, he committed suicide. After Duncan's death, Annabelle became convinced that her personal maid Phebe knew of the affair with Cass and the reason for Duncan's suicide. To keep her from revealing her knowledge, Annabelle sold her down the river. Only then, Cass writes in his diary, does he realize the full impact of his "single act of sin and perfidy. . . . I suddenly felt the world outside of me was shifting" and that a "process of general disintegration," of which he was the center, had only begun. "[I]t was as though," Cass concludes, "the vibration set up in the whole fabric of the world by my act had spread infinitely and with ever increasing power, and no man could know the end" (189).

A man of tradition, Cass acts predictably in the face of the great tragedy caused by a single act of his. He goes home, frees his slaves, joins the Confederate Army when the Civil War breaks out, and though he constantly exposed himself to danger, refuses to fire a shot in retaliation. Finally he is killed in the battle of Atlanta. Cass's philosophy, which Bayard Sartoris and Lacy Buchan would understand and act upon, is succinctly expressed by one of the characters in Walker Percy's *The Moviegoer*. "All these years," Emily Cutrer says, "I have been assuming . . . that among certain people, gentlefolk I don't mind calling them, there exists a certain set of meanings held in common, that a certain manner and a certain grace come as naturally as breathing." The people of her class, she continues, think they are better than ordinary people because "we do not shirk our obligations either to ourselves or to others." When Bayard Sartoris returns the passionate embrace of his stepmother, he knows he has violated the code of acceptable behavior; therefore he has to accept the consequences of his actions. Cass's reactions to violating the trust of a friend are the same. Not only will he accept the full responsibility for his act of "sin and perfidy"; he accepts the ever-increasing waves of disaster that result from his initial act. He has taken the life of a friend and submitted an innocent slave girl to unimaginable horror; therefore he will not take another life, even in war, because he has "used up . . . his right for blood" (198). Years after Jack Burden has rejected Anne Stanton's offer of her body, he observes: "My nobility (or whatever it was) had had in my world almost as dire a consequence as Cass Mastern's sin had had in his. Which may tell something about two worlds" (297). Jack's "nobility," his inability to act with head and heart simultaneously, set in motion a chain of events that take the lives of Willie Stark and Adam Stanton and almost destroy Anne and him.

When Jack is convinced that he cannot understand Cass Mastern, he drops out of graduate school, begins working on the *Chronicle* and after a time marries Lois: "As long as I regarded Lois as a beautiful, juicy, soft, vibrant, sweet-smelling, sweet-breathed machine for provoking and satisfying the appetite (and that was the Lois I had married), all was well. But as soon as I began to regard her as a person, trouble began. All would have been well, perhaps, had Lois been struck dumb at puberty. Then no man could have withstood her" (321–22). Unfortunately for their relationship, Lois can talk, and as soon as Jack begins to "realize that the noises she made with her mouth resembled human speech and were more than rudimentary demands for, or expressions of gratifications at, food or copulation, a certain resistance began to grow" in him (322).

Although Jack is sorry, he insists, for what he has done to her, he begins gradually to withdraw from their relationship. Then he reverts to the procedure he always follows when he is confronted with a problem for which he knows no simple solution. It had served him well when he could not determine why Cass Mastern acted as he did. It is, he said, a precious heritage from his mother who is forever trying to make "a little island right in the middle of time," an attempt to solve a problem by refusing to confront it. It is what Jack refers to as the Big Sleep:

> He would sleep twelve hours, fourteen hours, fifteen hours, feeling himself, while asleep plunge deeper and deeper into sleep like a diver groping downward into dark water feeling for something which may be there and which would glitter if there were any light in the depth, but there isn't any light. Then in the morning he would lie in bed, not wanting anything, not even hungry, hearing the small sounds of the world sneaking and seeping back into the room, under the door, through the glass, through the cracks in the wall, through the very pores of the wood and plaster. Then he would think: *if I don't get up, I can't go back to bed.* (201)

Then one day he goes back into the world, to face the world as well as an emotional and intellectual cripple can. In Jack's every act in the novel so far, he has succeeded only in alienating himself further from the world in which he must live. He has cut himself off from home and friends (his mother and Burden's Landing), from human love (Anne Stanton), from the past and its traditions (Cass Mastern), even from the world of sensory pleasures (Lois). Finally he comes to a state of almost complete isolation, to the hotel room "where nothing was mine and nothing knew my name, and nothing had a thing to say to me about anything that had ever happened." He is modern man, caught up in "time's monotone," in Allen Tate's phrase, one who has cut "himself off from the past, and without the benefit of the fund of traditional wisdom approaches the simplest problems of life as if nobody had ever heard of them before."[3] His life is still without aim or purpose; although he is constantly in motion, now that he has re-entered the world, his energy is unfocused. Like the blind crab in Tate's "Ode to the Confederate Dead," his life is filled with motion, but it has no direction, for there is no "purposeful world" in which he can expend his energy. In this state he accepts a position with the new governor of the state, a man who, because he had the courage to buck the political machine, has progressed very quickly from "Cousin Willie from the Country" with "The Christmas tie" to "the Boss," the most powerful man in the state. Although Jack recognizes Willie for the demagogue he is, Stark is the only person he knows who is aware of what he wants and how to get it. Willie's success is the result of what he would no doubt call a realistic view of the world, but we know, as Warren suggests in the introduction to the Modern Library edition of the novel, that Willie's considerable accomplishments come from the expertise with which he applies modern remedies to old problems— pragmatism, utilitarianism, positivism, mechanism, behaviorism. (vi) The basic problem demanding these new remedies Willie Stark could have learned in his Presbyterian Sunday School classes: it concerns the nature of man. "Man is conceived in sin and born in corruption," he tells Jack Burden on more than one occasion, "and he passeth from the stink of the didie to the stench of the shroud" (49). Given man with

3 Allen Tate, *Essays of Four Decades* (New York: William Morrow, 1968), 539.

his propensity for evil, one can imagine the kind of society he would build if his actions were not closely regulated. "You've got to *use* fellows like Bryan and Tiny Duffy, and that scum down in the Legislature," Stark tells his idealistic attorney general, Hugh Miller. "You can't make bricks without straw, and most of the time all the straw you get is second-hand straw from the cowpen. And if you think you can make it different, you're crazy as a hoot owl" (146; emphasis mine).

Since man is depraved and the material out of which he must create the forms of society is defiled, what can a man do who would like to bring about social improvement? All he can do, Stark insists, is to try. He must never cease to struggle. The important thing is what the man who has the power to effect change does with the dirt:

> "Dirt's a funny thing," the Boss said. "Come to think of it, there ain't a thing but dirt on this green God's globe except what's under water, and that's dirt too. It's dirt makes the grass grow. A diamond ain't a thing in the world but a piece of dirt that got awful hot. And God-a-Mighty picked up a handful of dirt and blew on it and made you and me and George Washington and mankind blessed in faculty and apprehension. It all depends on what you do with the dirt." (50)

The obvious question, then, is what *do* you do with the dirt? Well, Stark says, you make goodness out of it. If you want it, you must make it, and the only thing you have to make it out of is badness. Social improvement, then, does not come from what Ransom would call the aesthetic forms. The customs, manners, habits, rituals, and ceremonies of the Stantons, the Burdens, and the Irwins are not the means by which civilization is effected. Good must be *created* by imperfect men out of tainted materials. If this is an accurate description of the state of the world, Willie is asked, how can one differentiate between the good and bad, how does one know that which he has created is really good? There are no absolute standards, Willie responds; therefore there is no universal good. That is good which meets the needs of a particular mo-

ment. "When your great-great-grandpappy climbed down out
of the tree," Stark tells Adam Stanton, "he didn't have any
more notion of good or bad, or right or wrong, than the hoot
owl that stayed up in the tree. Well, he climbed down and he
began to make up Good as he went along" (273). That which
man named good was what he needed to regulate the economic order. The definition of what is good or right changes
as man's economic needs vary.

If one accepts this attitude, if there can be no fixed notion
of right and wrong, if good varies with the practical needs of
the moment, what restrains man's selfish impulses? If social
traditions are mere hindrances to bringing about much needed
changes, how is imperfect man able to confine his activities to
the channels of acceptable behavior? Again, Stark's answer is
explicit. The only reason man acts as a man and not as a beast
is his fear of the law, and even the law is often inadequate:

> "I can see [Stark says] what the law is like. It's like a single-bed blan-
> ket on a double bed and three folks in the bed and a cold night. There
> ain't ever enough blanket to cover the case, no matter how much pull-
> ing and hauling, and somebody is always going to nigh catch pneumo-
> nia. Hell, the law is like the pants you bought last year for a growing
> boy, but it is always this year and the seams are popped and the shank-
> bone's to the breeze. The law is always too short and too tight for
> growing human-kind. The best you can do is do something and then
> make up some law to fit and by the time that law gets on the books you
> would have done something different." (145)

From these examples of Willie Stark's basic attitudes, one
can well understand Warren's denial that he was attempting
to write a fictional biography of Huey P. Long. Instead he
was presenting a broad spectrum of modern attitudes, and
William James was probably the central figure that lay behind the creation of Willie Stark.[4] To Willie Stark there are no
absolute values. There is no undeviating standard by which

4 Warren, Introduction, *All the King's Men* (New York: Modern Library, 1953),
   vi.

man can determine the rightness or wrongness of an action. All values are relative and man should be concerned only with results, never processes. Since the desired end-product justifies any means necessary to produce it, to complain about the corruption and graft of a political machine, Stark insists, is unrealistic and just plain stupid:

> "More money for graft the opposition always screamed. Sure . . . [Stark says] there's some graft, but there's just enough to make the wheels turn without squeaking. And remember this. There never was a machine rigged up by man didn't represent some loss of energy. How much energy do you get out of a lump of coal when you run a steam dynamo or a locomotive compared to what there is in that lump of coal? Damned little. Well we do a hell of a lot better than the best dynamo or locomotive ever invented. Sure I've got a bunch of crooks around here, but they're too lily-livered to get very crooked. I've got my eye on 'em. And I do deliver the state something. I damn well do." (417)

What one must do is to measure the effectiveness of Stark's administration. Is what he produces for the state worth more than it costs to make it? If so, then he is, as he says, "making good out of evil." He is giving the people roads to get their crops to market, free bridges across the rivers, affordable hospital care, and free public education. He can accomplish these things because he is able to attract the support of the "hicks" and the "red necks" with such slogans as "soak the rich," and by building a strong political machine comprised of wise and practical manipulators (like Sadie Burke), idealists (Hugh Miller), trained publicists and researchers (Jack Burden), and opportunists (Tiny Duffy).

Jack's decision to go to work for the man who believes in the "moral neutrality of history" and the "theory of historical costs" is perhaps his first positive action in the novel. He has been unable to act, because there seems to be nothing worth doing; even his not taking Anne Stanton was merely an "echo of an old honor." Although his commitment to Willie is not complete—he is able to detect, he says, Willie's inability to differentiate between his greatness and his ungreatness—he does his work thoroughly and well. A trained researcher, he uses his skills to find the skeletons in the closets of Willie's enemies. Occasionally he becomes listless, loses his motivation for action, and drops temporarily into the Big Sleep. These relapses, however, occur infrequently and soon pass; then Jack returns to Willie, protesting his neutrality and insisting that he is his own man, not another of Willie's hired hands. "I'm not one of your scum," he tells Stark, "and I'm still grinning when I please." At any rate, he reasons, he is an idealist and doesn't have to believe in the significance of what he is doing.

Jack's neutrality, which is becoming more suspect as the novel progresses, is finally destroyed by the repercussions of his second piece of historical research. Willie has told Jack to find the truth of Judge Irwin's background, that which he does not want known. Despite Jack's protest that there are no unsavory episodes in Irwin's past, Stark insists "there is always something." After months of following false leads and accomplishing nothing, Jack finally discovers that Irwin's fortune came from stock in a utility company he neglected to prosecute for tax evasion while he was attorney general. When he was appointed legal counsel and vice-president of the firm, the man he replaced was so dejected that he committed suicide. Although Governor Stanton was aware of Irwin's duplicity, he did not act on his information. He did not even reveal what he knew to his old friend.

The repercussions of Jack's second journey into the past are many and profound. Willie Stark has been trying to get Adam Stanton—another modern who dismisses the world when it fails to coincide with his image of how it should be—to become director of the hospital he is building as a lasting symbol of his importance to the people of the state. Adam Stanton is one of a type that figures prominently in Warren's imaginative vision, according to Victor Strandberg, "Warren's

clean people who refuse passage into a polluted and compro-
mised adult environment." [5] Willie wants his hospital to be as
nearly perfect as it can be—he denies his avowed relativism
by refusing to appoint a crooked contractor to build it—and
he wants the best doctor he knows, Adam Stanton, to head it.
When Adam is not persuaded by Jack's version of Willie's
argument that good can come out of evil, Jack shows him and
Anne photostats of the information he has uncovered linking
their father to Judge Irwin's crime. Adam capitulates, allowing himself to be persuaded by Willie's insistence that he will
have a free hand in the operation of the hospital and that much
good can be done there. The effect on Anne is more traumatic.
After three engagements but no marriages, she has settled in
the city to be near Adam and to do some work for charity.
Her work for the Children's Home has necessitated that she
meet Willie, and she has been attracted to him—apparently
finding in him the singleness of purpose she did not find in
Jack—and now that her illusions about her father have been
destroyed, she becomes Willie's mistress.

Jack says her relationship with Willie Stark "betrayed an
idea of mine which had . . . more importance for me" than he
had ever realized; so again he reverts to the Big Sleep. This
time he will escape through the Journey West, for a part of the
American Dream is that one can get a new start in the West:
"For West is where we all plan to go someday. It is where you
go when the land gives out and the old field pines encroach. It
is where you go when you get the letter saying: *Flee, all is discovered.* It is where you go when you look down at the blade
in your hand and see the blood on it. It is where you go when
you are told that you are a bubble on the tide of empire. It is
where you go when you hear that thar's gold in them-thar
hills" (286). Jack realizes that the philosophy of assumed
neutrality, made with his head but not carried to his heart,

5 Victor Strandberg, *The Poetic Vision of Robert Penn Warren* (Lexington: University Press of Kentucky, 1977), 122.

like that of Jacob Horner in Barth's *The End of the Road*, is not adequate to deal with personal relationships. He tries to have the magic of western expansion work for him. He flees to the West:

> For that is where you came after you have crossed oceans and eaten stale biscuits while prisoned forty days and nights in a stormy-tossed rat-trap, after you have sweated in the greenery and heard the savage whoop, after you have built cabins and cities and bridged rivers, after you have lain with women and scattered children like millet seed in a high wind, after you have composed resonant documents, made noble speeches, and bathed your arms in blood to the elbows, after you have shaken with malaria in the marshes and in the icy wind across the high plains. That is where you come, to lie alone on a bed in a hotel room in Long Beach, California. Where I lay, while outside my window a neon sign flickered on and off to the time of my heart, systole and diastole, flushing and flushing again the gray sea mist with a tint like blood. (327)

Although he lies there on his hotel bed, "having drowned in the West" and his body "having drifted down" to lie in the "subliminal ooze of the sea flood of history," the pain remains. Neither the magic of the Journey West nor the peace of unconsciousness produced by the Big Sleep can erase from his mind the image of a girl floating face upward in the sea with a single white gull flying high over her, nor can he forget how this same girl looked with her head reclining against the seat of an open roadster with the moonlight fingering her closed eyelids. He has sacrificed an image of an idealized past, and he cannot make himself believe the girl he had known a long time back had been merely "smooth-faced and healthy" and not "beautiful and charming"; neither can he accept the suggestion that he had been "tormented by a mysterious itch" that went by the word *love*. He has handed Anne Stanton to Willie Stark, and that fact is too horrible to face because it has robbed him "of something out of the past" which, until then, "unwittingly" he had been living.

His Journey West, however, does pay off, for there "at the

end of History, the Last Man on the Last Coast," he moves from one stage of his philosophic development to another. Although the Big Sleep is no longer soothing and satisfying, he discovers a dream: "That dream was the dream that all life is but the dark heave of blood and the twitch of the nerve. . . . It was bracing because after that dream I felt that in a way, Anne Stanton did not exist. The words *Anne Stanton* were simply a name for a peculiarly complicated piece of mechanism which should mean nothing whatsoever to Jack Burden, who himself was simply another rather complicated piece of mechanism" (329). He knows that any place to which he flees will be like the one he left so he is ready to go back to the man who is making good out of evil. The difference is that now he is a pragmatist and a positivist. His relativism is born in the bright glitter of the sun of everydayness, the same light that ·has destroyed the last faint glimmer of his idealism. He and Willie are now as one; the attempts at forced neutrality are no longer necessary.

On his way back to join Stark, Jack finds a name for his philosophic creed. In a gas station in Don Jon, New Mexico, he talks to a man standing on the side of a service station:

> He was an old fellow, seventy-five if a day, with a face like sun-brittled leather and pale-blue eyes under the brim of a felt hat which had once been black. The only thing remarkable about him was the fact that while you looked into the sun-brittled leather of the face, which seemed as stiff and devitalized as the hide on a mummy's jaw, you would suddenly see a twitch in the left cheek, up toward the pale-blue eye. You would think he was going to wink, but he wasn't going to wink. The twitch was simply an independent phenomenon, unrelated to the face or to what was behind the face or to the whole tissue of phenomena which is the world we are lost in. (332–33)

Jack, then, falls headlong into mechanism. He takes comfort in the conviction that he had no more control over what happened between Anne Stanton and Willie Stark than the old man has over the twitch in his face. One cannot order the circumstances of his daily life, for existence is merely stimulus and response: "The twitch in the leg of the dead frog in the laboratory when a charge of electricity is passed through it." There is neither good nor evil, only the automatic acts of the machine. Jack can now enter into his world with enthusiasm, for, as Robert B. Heilman says, no longer are there "reservations nibbling at the edge of his apparently whole-souled commitment."[6] Jack says he feels "clean and free" because he has found the great secret of the universe; he feels as one with the Great Twitch.

Judge Irwin's reaction to the information is not at all what Jack had expected. Although Judge Irwin knows he can keep Jack from revealing his information to Stark, like Cass Mastern he is determined to take full responsibility for his actions. Such an attitude in no way meshes with Jack's idea of the Great Twitch. So after revealing the facts he has uncovered and being completely disarmed by the Judge's reaction, Jack goes home to take a nap, only to be awakened by his mother screaming, "You killed him!" His mother's cry moves him into another philosophic attitude, just as the Journey West had provoked his abandonment of the Big Sleep and his acceptance of the Great Twitch. Later he learns from the doctor that immediately after Jack left the house the Judge shot himself cleanly through the heart, and from his mother he discovers that the Judge, the only man she had ever loved, was Jack's father. A little later Tom Stark, Willie's only son, dies as a result of an injury he had received on the football field. In order to discover the past, as one critic has pointed out, Jack has to kill his father. "Searching for the future," Robert B. Heilman says, "Willie may be said to have killed his son."[7]

After Tom is injured and Willie has to allow politics to taint the building of the hospital that was to perpetuate his memory, Stark loses his motivation for action. He tells Sadie

6 Heilman, "Melpomene as Wallflower," 93.
7 *Ibid.*

Burke, who has been his mistress for years, that he is leaving her and going back to his wife. In a fit of pique and jealousy, Sadie tells Tiny Duffy that Anne Stanton has been Willie's mistress. Adam Stanton, the idealist, the man of idea who has reduced life to abstractions, and one who believes in removal at any cost of that which disturbs his view of reality, resorts to violence when Tiny tells him of Anne's relationship with Willie. Adam shoots Willie down in the capitol, and is killed by Sugar Boy, Willie's chauffeur and bodyguard. Willie dies a few days later, and his last words are, "It might have all been different, Jack. . . . You got to believe that." Willie Stark waited too late to attempt to alter the course of his life. Too late he becomes aware of the inadequacy of fact alone. Facts should be irretrievably tied to ideas, for without ideas that, as Richard Weaver says, do have consequences, man is incomplete; Willie is modern man, broken into many pieces, and no one can put him back together again.

Jack Burden, who has been at different times both the man of idea and the man of fact, learns of their necessary fusion. He moves finally toward grounding his world view in theological belief. He learns that the essence of the past is recoverable, that he must accept the necessity of an imperfect world, one of which evil will always be an essential part, that the world—present, past, and future—"is all of a piece." This view is expressed in a combination of pragmatism and idealism, of facts and ideas, that he calls the "spider web" theory, and with this discovery he can understand for the first time why Judge Irwin and Cass Mastern acted as they did:

> Cass Mastern lived for a few years and in that time he learned that the world is all of one piece. He learned that the world is like an enormous spider web and if you touch it, however lightly, at any point, the vibration ripples to the remotest perimeter and the drowsy spider feels the tingle and is drowsy no more but springs out to fling the gossamer coils about you who have touched the web and then inject the black, numbing poison under your hide. It does not matter whether or not

you meant to brush the web of things. Your happy foot or your gay wing may have brushed it ever so lightly, but what happens always happens and there is the spider, bearded black and with his great faceted eyes glittering like mirrors in the sun, or like God's eye, and the fangs dripping. (200–201)

When Jack first learns of Cass Mastern's actions after his friend's suicide and Phebe's being sold, he cannot accept what he has learned because to him, Warren says, "The world was simply an accumulation of items, odds and ends of things like the broken and misused and dust-shrouded things gathered in a garret. Or it was a flux of things before his eyes (or behind his eyes) and one thing had nothing to do, in the end with anything else." With this view of the world that we are "prisoners in," Jack cannot understand Mastern's sense of guilt. Only later Warren says, when he learned that the world is "all of one piece," did Cass Mastern's destructive feeling of responsibility for the repercussions of his own actions make any sense to him. In one of his most helpful essays for readers of his fiction, Warren provides further insight into the reasons for Burden's altered view of his relationship to the world: "[Man is] in the world with continual and intimate interpenetration, an inevitable osmosis of being which in the end . . . affirms his identity." [8]

Jack learns one of the paradoxes of life: no event is real when taken alone, but it receives its reality from other events which in isolation are just as unreal. This principle affirms that our own identity is dependent upon direction, movement, relationships. Life, then, involves, Jack learns, a search for truth. At first he felt that if he would know the truth he must divest himself of the entanglements of the past—of home, family, and friends—of the traditional values of the society that produced him. Then he learns that the freedom he thinks he has earned by becoming anyone, anywhere, is not real. He

8 Warren, "Knowledge and the Image of Man," in *Robert Penn Warren: A Collection of Critical Essays*, 241.

has not dissolved the long-established personal relationship with Anne Stanton, with whom he was once in love; he cannot erase images of her as girl and woman from his mind. When he is convinced that he is responsible for the capitulation of Anne to Willie Stark, he can only relieve his feelings of guilt by joining Willie in his pragmatic world view. Later, Jack's quest for knowledge uncovered the fact that Willie Stark and Adam Stanton were doomed to destroy each other, each sought the completion of an incomplete self in the other, each yearning toward and trying to become the other. Because of the "terrible division of their age," however, the "man of fact and the man of idea" would inevitably destroy each other. Jack learns, nevertheless, that they were not doomed under the godhead of the "Great Twitch." They lived in the agony of will, because though "history is blind man is not."

With this conviction Jack moves from an awareness of the facts of case histories to a knowledge of the truth of history. From this truth Jack acquires a faith; not only does he know that he is responsible for the results of his actions, whether intended or not, he also comes to believe in a metaphysical reality that justifies the existence of evil in the world. As the Scholarly Attorney, now living with Jack and Anne, approaches death, he dictates to Jack the essence of his belief, and Jack says he is not certain that, in his own way, he does not believe the old man's creed:

> The creation of man whom God in His foreknowledge knew doomed to sin was the awful index of God's omnipotence. For it would have been a thing of trifling and contemptible ease for Perfection to create mere perfection. To do so would, to speak truth, be not creation but extension. Separateness is identity and the only way for God to create, truly create, man was to make him separate from God Himself, and to be separate from God is to be sinful. The creation of evil is therefore the index of God's glory and His power. That had to be so that the creation of good might be the index of man's glory and power. But by God's help. By His help and in His wisdom. (462)

Though Jack Burden's faith is not the orthodox Christian

one, his search through his "personal past and the past that lies behind that personal past" has given him a glimpse of metaphysical reality. By combining the two facets of his temperament—fact and idea—he has unified the division that destroyed his two friends, Adam Stanton and Willie Stark. He realizes that he is involved in the process through which an action is achieved, as he is in the results of that action. Now he and Anne can cut their physical ties with Burden's Landing, but they will come back to watch the youngsters play tennis and swim in the gulf, for in them they will see former manifestations of themselves. Now, they go to face the convulsion of the world, however, because for the first time Jack is prepared to move "out of history into history and the awful responsibility of time."

V Social Forms and Social Order: Eudora Welty's The Optimist's Daughter

Eudora Welty's *The Optimist's Daughter* (1969) is an effectively understated delineation of why it is impossible for anyone to be absolutely certain that he fully understands the nature and importance of human actions and experiences. It is very difficult, if not impossible, for one to know the reasons motivating a human being, even a close relative, to commit a particular act. One cannot conceive of the exact nature of the relationship that exists between two individuals, regardless of how well he knows those two persons. He cannot be sure of his feelings toward the community in which he grew up, toward friends and relatives who still live there. These are the kinds of problems with which Eudora Welty is concerned in *The Optimist's Daughter*: Laurel's attempts to come to terms with her father's death; with Fay Chisom, the underbred woman who is her father's second wife; with her own early marriage and the death of her husband; with the precise nature of the relationship between father and mother, not to mention Laurel's feelings toward Mount Salus, the community in which she grew up, and its inhabitants.

Confronted as she is with all of these problems, which she struggles desperately to solve, Laurel's difficulties are compounded by her discovery that everything about her hometown does not fit the abstract conception of it she has always cherished. Maybe it once was as she conceived it to be, but she and Mount Salus have both changed. Her being at home and trying to solve her problems there compound her difficulty. The social fabric of a particular community, toward which she has long held certain fixed attitudes, multiplies her difficulties. Phenomena that seem to submit to obvious explanations assume confusing dimensions. Laurel's probing of complicated human relationships lead her far beyond her powers of comprehension because of the setting in which her deeply disturbing, soul searching analyses occur, the once familiar but now strange village of Mount Salus, with its apparently tragically flawed citizens, customs, and ceremonies. Laurel's traumatic experience is related in Miss Welty's inimitable manner—a devastating serious human dilemma presented in an amusing, often disarmingly humorous manner. Her ear for the rhythms of southern speech and her understanding of the nuances of rural behavior are seldom more convincingly portrayed than in this novel.

In one of her essays Eudora Welty comments on the craft of writing: "[T]he business of writing, and the responsibility of the writer, is to disentangle the significant—in character, incident, setting, mood, everything—from the random and meaningless and irrelevant that in real life surround and beset it. It is a matter of his selecting and, by all that implies, of changing 'real' life as he goes. . . . He makes choices at the explicit demand of this one present story . . . . No two stories ever go the same way." [1] In spite of Miss Welty's warning, however, some readers were not prepared for *The Optimist's Daughter*, coming as it does on the heels of *Losing Battles*. If the latter novel is deceptively complex, as Louis D. Rubin, Jr., has said, because "everything is contained right there on the surface," *The Optimist's Daughter* is deceptively simple be-

---

[1] Eudora Welty, *The Eye of the Story* (New York: Random House, 1978), 120.

cause hardly anything lies on the surface. Its literal meaning seems simple enough: Laurel McKelva Hand, a sophisticated young woman from Chicago, who has come to New Orleans to visit her hospitalized father, is repelled by his crude and self-centered second wife, and tries to decide why her father married this woman. The second wife, Fay Chisom, is as much unlike Laurel's mother (the first wife, Becky) as any human being could possibly be, and no explanation for her father's second marriage can be completely satisfactory to Laurel. Her bewilderment continues unabated despite the explanations offered: an old man deluded by youthful energy and vitality, he enjoyed having someone to spoil; his "having her gave him something to live for." Neither can Laurel accept the accusations of one of the neighbors in Mount Salus, Mississippi, Judge McKelva's home and the community in which Laurel grew up. After her husband had been killed in World War II, if Laurel, as Miss Tennyson Bullock suggests half-seriously, had come back to live in Mount Salus, her father would have had no reason to marry Fay. All these explanations are partially true but none, we learn near the end of the story, contains the whole truth. Whatever our opinion of *Losing Battles*, it is increasingly apparent as we read *The Optimist's Daughter* that the meaning of the latter is not contained in an opaque surface level. This story is simply, and apparently straightforwardly, told by an omniscient narrator who carefully releases the essential facts of the narrative as she wants us to have them. The tightly structured story, which is divided into three almost equal parts and a brief conclusion, demonstrates the firm control that a master craftsman can exercise over her material. Each part is built upon information given previously, apparently with nothing withheld, but only as the novel comes to a close, in a manner as quiet and natural as the sun sets or the day breaks, are we aware of the complexities of the human relationships with which we have been intimately involved. As the good artist always can,

Miss Welty has let us share her characters' experiences, permitted us to learn as they do until finally we know them better than we know our closest acquaintances, perhaps better than the characters know themselves.

The narrative technique employed in this novel is much like that used by Jane Austen in *Emma*. Wayne Booth has explained how in that novel Jane Austen controls our reactions to Emma: "By showing most of the story through Emma's eyes, the author insures that we shall travel with Emma rather than stand against her. It is not simply that Emma provides, in the unimpeachable evidence of her own conscience, proof that she has redeeming qualities that do not appear on the surface." The danger in using such a technique, Booth continues, is that the reader in the end may overlook some of Emma's mistakes since each of them is reported unobtrusively as it occurs. Booth explains there is also another danger involved in using this manner of narration: "On the one hand she cares about maintaining some sense of mystery as long as she can. On the other, she works at all points to heighten the reader's sense of dramatic irony." In practice, however, one effect tends to cancel out the other: "whatever effects are taken to mystify inevitably decrease the dramatic irony, and, whenever dramatic irony is increased . . . mystery is inevitably destroyed." (Wayne C. Booth, *The Rhetoric of Fiction*, [Chicago: The University of Chicago Press, 1961], 255.)

The Optimist's Daughter is told in a similar manner, by an omniscient narrator who chooses to view most events from the point of view of Laurel. Laurel is a deeply troubled young woman, but we don't know how severely disturbed she is until the story ends and we realize how badly she has distorted some of the early episodes, until we realize she is emotionally incapable of reacting to them. Miss Welty, it seems to me, succeeds admirably in handling the difficulties involved in using this method of narration. Although the reader is aware that his and Laurel's reaction to Fay's insufferable behavior is virtually the same, dramatic irony is maintained because there is an obvious difference between the reader's and Laurel's reaction to the Dalzells episode and to the lengthy wake and burial scene. One of the chief virtues of the novel, I think, is the skillful manner in which Miss Welty has managed to achieve and maintain both a sense of mystery and the effect of dramatic irony. In an attempt to demonstrate the quality of Miss Welty's artistry, I have chosen to stay, in the beginning at least, closely to the details of the action as Laurel sees it. In this way we can remain true to Miss Welty's intentions: that the nature and extent of Laurel's alienation be revealed gradually and naturally as we experience with her the thoughts and feelings that engage her; at the same time we are aware that we know more than she does about what is going on.

All the McKelvas are in New Orleans because the judge has come to consult an eye specialist, Dr. Nate Courtland, a man near Laurel's age who grew up next door to her in Mount Salus. The result of Dr. Courtland's examination is the discovery that Judge McKelva has a slipped retina and needs an immediate operation. Although Dr. Courtland does not want to do the operation—he has known the judge all of his life (the judge has helped pay his expenses through medical school) and he fears that he cannot maintain a position of proper detachment—the judge insists: "Nate," he says: "I hied myself away from home and comfort and tracked down here and put myself in your hands for one simple reason: I've got confidence in you. Now show me I'm not too old to exercise good judgment." [2] So the matter is settled and the operation is scheduled.

When the question of an operation first is broached, Fay becomes aware that she, the wife, is not being consulted. "Isn't my vote going to count at all?" she asks. That she is being ignored, however, is not the only thing that's troubling

2 Eudora Welty, *The Optimist's Daughter* (New York: Random House, 1972), 10. All references are to this edition, and page numbers will be given in the text.

her. When she first learns her husband must undergo an operation, she complains: "I don't see why this had to happen to *me*." And immediately after the operation, while she and Laurel are waiting for the judge to be brought to his room, she exclaims: "What a way to keep his promise. When he told me he would bring me to New Orleans some day, it was to see the Carnival. . . . And the Carnival's going on right now. It looks as if this is as close as we'll get to a parade" (12–13). When the judge is back in his room and coming out from under the influence of the ether, he asks Laurel, using her childhood name, "Eh, Polly? . . . What's your mother have to say about me?" (15). Before Laurel can answer Fay leaps up from the bed where she has been lying (the judge is in a double room) rushes to the judge's bed, and shouts: "'Look-a-here. . . . Who's this?' She pointed to the gold button over her breastbone" (15).

Important family concerns are being settled and she is being excluded. She is resentful, as she naturally would be, but her crude, selfish behavior reveals, without comment from the narrator, the essentials of her character. As we come to know Fay and Laurel better, these remarks will take on additional layers of meaning, and Laurel's reactions to them will help us understand better her troubled state of mind.

As Laurel has telephoned her office and reported that she will not return immediately, she and Fay take lodging at the Hibiscus, "a decaying mansion on a changing street." Because of their schedules at the hospital, Fay and Laurel are seldom at the boardinghouse at the same time except to sleep. Although they are separated only by a thin partition of wallboard, there is no communication between the two. "Where there was no intimacy," the narrator explains, "Laurel shrank from contact: she shrank from that thin board and from the vague apprehension that some night she might hear Fay cry or laugh like a stranger at something she herself would rather not know" (18).

What is Laurel afraid of learning from Fay? Why the judge married her? Is there something about her father that she is attempting to block from her consciousness? The reader is not to know yet and he has little time to ponder these questions, because Miss Welty's story moves steadily on. Because she knows he had loved to be read to once—What? By whom? —Laurel secures copies of her father's favorite detective novels and begins to read to him. While he lies quietly and gives little appearance of being aware of her presence, "Pity stabbed at her. Did they *move too fast* for him now?" Hoping to find something that will interest him more, she buys a second-hand copy of *Nicholas Nickleby* and begins to read from it. The result is about the same; he lies quietly with his eyes closed and only speaks to ask her to continue reading when she stops. "What occupied his full mind," Laurel concludes, "was time itself; time passing; he was concentrating" (19). One wonders, of course: What is he concentrating on? His impending death? Has he only now come to realize his basic relationship to passing time?

As Judge McKelva is devoting his complete attention to the last days of his life, a new patient is moved into his room, an old man named Dalzell, blind and nearly deaf. Mr. Dalzell, a fellow Mississippian, is awaiting a cancer operation, but he quickly decides that Judge McKelva is his son Archie Lee. "Archie Lee," he yells, "I might've known if you ever did come home, you'd come home drunk" (21). With the head of the clan incapacitated, all the Dalzells, including Archie Lee, have gathered to pay their respects as the old man's life comes to an end. Mr. Dalzell lies in his bed awaiting his turn at the operating room and yelling instructions to his son: "Archie Lee, you gonna load that gun or you rather be caught napping?" or "You got that gun loaded yet? Archie Lee, I declare, I want to see you load that gun before they start coming" (23). Finally the orderlies come for him and as they wheel him down the hall toward the operating room, he is yelling, "*Told* you rascals not to let the fire go out." While he was undergoing a useless operation—we know his cancer is terminal—his daughter, the son, Archie Lee, and Dalzells of all ages are in the waiting room. Around one large table are five grown men and women, obviously the old man's grandchildren, and nearby are an older woman, apparently their mother, and her brother, Archie Lee. "Their coats were on the table in a heap together, and open shoeboxes and paper sacks stood about on the floor; they were a family in the middle of their supper." They are here as a family in a meaningful kind of ritual to demonstrate their affection for their dying father and grand-father. Because they are a family, their shared grief makes them a community of mourners and allows them through participation in a social occasion with a definitely fixed order to divert their attention from their own mortality, the awe-some certainty of death; they are able to objectify their feel-ings, as Laurel is not. (Neither can Judge McKelva, of course, but such grave rites are not intended for the victim but for the bereaved; the dying man is left to "brood on the riddle of mor-tality.") Unlike the Dalzells, Laurel feels, as Allen Tate says of George Posey, "the shock of the world" at the end of her nerves. Although we do not know the extent to which Laurel has been affected by the death of her husband and mother, and by her father's remarriage, we do know that her inability to feel genuine human emotion, and why, is a large part of the story that is gradually emerging.

As Mr. Dalzell's condition worsens, so does Judge Mc-Kelva's. But Laurel's conviction that her father's death is slowly but inevitably approaching, despite Dr. Courtland's assurance that the eye is healing normally, brings her no closer to her father or to Fay. Once she comes into her father's room when he is unaware of her presence and observes: "Her fa-ther's right arm was free of the cover and lay out on the bed. It was bare to the shoulder, its skin soft and gathered, like a woman's sleeve. It showed her he was no longer concentrating" (33). Right then, with his mind no longer on his own mortality, she knew he was dying, for "his whole pillowless head went dusky, as if he had laid it under the surface of dark, pouring water and held it there." Even after Dr. Courtland rushes into the room, at the nurse's bidding, and begins searching for Judge McKelva's pulse and listening for his heartbeat, Laurel looks on, half realizing what she is observing: "It was her father who appeared to Laurel as the one listening. His upper lip had lifted, short and soft as a child's, showing ghostly-pale teeth which no one ever saw when he spoke or laughed. It gave him the smile of a child who is hiding in the dark while others hunt him, waiting to be found" (34). (We wonder if he is still optimistic?) What Miss Welty is saying, too, is that Judge McKelva is not the only character with impaired vision. Laurel's inability to perceive her father's need for someone to share his final agonies has not allowed her to participate in his thoughts and feelings during his last illness. Only at his death are we finally aware that the alienation of father and daughter is not a recent development. Only after layer upon layer of natural but apparently not particularly significant action has been related will the reason for this separation be fully understood. Only near the end of the novel will the meaning of its title become apparent.

As her husband's condition deteriorates, Fay's egotism becomes more obvious. "About ready to get up, hon?" she asks the judge. "Listen, they're holding parades out yonder right now. . . . What's the good of a Carnival if we don't get to go, hon?" (26) At one point, Laurel thinks that she and Fay should get better acquainted, at least to make the pretense at being a family, but when Laurel knocks on Fay's door at the Hibiscus, she is greeted with "What do you want?" Laurel entered Fay's narrow half-room, and in an attempt to get a conversation going—she wants to know her stepmother better she tells herself—she asks Fay about her family. "My family?" Fay responds. "None of 'em living. That's why I ever left Texas and came to Mississippi." "Oh I wouldn't have run off and left anybody that needed me," she continues, revealing more of Laurel's troubled conscience than she knows. "Just to call myself an artist and make a lot of money" (27–28). One night in her room at the Hibiscus, unable to sleep for some reason she does not understand, Laurel decides to go back to the hospital. As she enters her father's room, she hears a "tight little voice," Fay's, screaming, "I tell you enough is enough." Then, even higher, the voice yells, "This is my birthday." (Fay's actions throughout the novel are related so vividly that one is inclined to forget that Laurel is the optimist's daughter, that this is her story.) At that moment Laurel sees Mrs. Martello running from the nurse's station into the judge's room. The next instant she reappears, dragging Fay, who breaks away and runs screaming down the corridor colliding with Laurel on her way to the waiting room. "She laid hands on him! . . . She taken ahold of him. She was abusing him," Mrs. Martello explains. "What's the matter with that woman?" Mrs. Martello then asks, turning back to Judge McKelva, "Does she want to *ruin* your eye?" (32–33). (Fay later explains to Laurel her reasons for seizing and shaking the judge: "I wanted to get him up out of there, and start him paying a little attention to me for a change.") Soon after this scene Dr. Courtland comes into the waiting room, where Laurel and Fay are with the Dalzells, and reports that the judge is dead.

The next afternoon as the train moves slowly through the dark swamp surrounding Lake Pontchartrain, carrying the body back to Mount Salus, Laurel looks out the window of the compartment she is sharing with Fay and sees "a seagull . . . hanging with wings fixed, like a stopped clock on a wall." Language cannot describe more accurately the state of Laurel's feeling. Her emotions are suspended at some point between listlessness and despair.

2

John Crowe Ransom insisted that a civilized society hands down many forms that serve no utilitarian function. One of these forms is the ritualistic behavior of a traditional people in the face of death. "The religious society exists," Ransom writes in *The World's Body*, "in order to serve the man in this crisis. Freed from his desolation by its virtue, he is not obliged now to run and throw himself upon the body in an ecstasy of grief, nor to go apart and brood upon the riddle of mortality, which may be the way of madness. His action is through the form of a pageant of grief, which is lovingly staged and attended by the religious community." [3]

That the good citizens of Mount Salus are prepared to celebrate the achievements of their favorite son and to divert his daughter's attention from the "putrefying corpse" and the "riddle of mortality" is evident as soon as the train bearing Laurel, Fay, and the judge's body pulls into the station. In response to a telephone call from Dr. Courtland, the train is met by Miss Adele Courtland, the doctor's sister and Laurel's first-grade teacher, and by "all six of Laurel's bridesmaids, as they still called themselves." As Laurel moves from the arms of one bridesmaid to another, Fay asks, "What are you here for?" "We came to meet you," one of the ladies says, "And to take you home" (49). Fay knows no one has come to meet her and take her anywhere, but she is prepared for the next visitor. A businessman appears at Laurel's side saying, "Now what would you like done with your father?" Before Laurel can answer, Fay interrupts: "I'm Mrs. McKelva now. If you're

3 John Crowe Ransom, *The World's Body* (Baton Rouge: Louisiana State University Press, 1968), 35.

the undertaker do your business with me." He whisks Fay away toward his place of business—while his assistants collect the coffin—with the assurance, "I'll return this lady to you by-and-by."

A man of his word, Mr. Pitts, the undertaker, returns Fay to the McKelva home, where other friends are gathered to help the mourners bear their grief. "What are all these people doing in my house?" Fay yells as soon as she opens the door. "You've got pies three deep in the pantry, and an ice box ready to pop," one friend of the family assures her. "Well," Fay responds, "I didn't know I was giving a reception." "We're Laurel's friends, Fay," Tish Bullock reminds her. "The six of us right here, we were her bridesmaids." "A lot of good her bridesmaids will ever do me," Fay replies. "And who's making themselves at home in my parlor?" (53). When she is informed that these are the remaining members of Laurel's mother's garden club, she exclaims, "What's Becky's garden party got to do with me?" Then she sticks her head in the door and yells, "The funeral's not until tomorrow." Laurel can see that matters are getting out of hand—and perhaps she perceives, too, something of Fay's feeling of aloneness because this "pageant of grief" is composed of Laurel's and Becky's friends—so she comes up to Fay and says, "They're all Father's friends, Fay. They're exactly the ones he'd have counted on to be here in the house to meet us." "Well, it's evermore unfair," Fay cries; "I haven't got anybody to count on but me, myself and I" (54). After this outburst, she goes upstairs. Soon thereafter the other guests quietly and in some embarrassment slip away with the promise to return "first thing in the morning." Only Miss Courtland is left and she is in the kitchen, getting everything ready for the events of the next day. Laurel feels compelled to explain to Miss Adele what had happened in New Orleans, particularly since her brother had performed the operation. "What happened," she says, "was not to Father's eye at all. Father was going to see . . . . Dr. Courtland was

right about the eye. He did everything right. . . . What happened wasn't like what happened to Mother" (56). When
Miss Adele has finished in the kitchen and is preparing to leave
for her home next door, she says, "People live their own way,
and to a certain extent I almost believe they may die their
way."

Although we do not have enough information to know
how the judge's last illness and death differed from his first
wife's—the narrator is carefully dribbling out the essentials
of her story—we can speculate intelligently on the reasons
for Judge McKelva's strange behavior during his last days.
(He has to face finally the profound question of his own mortality.) Laurel goes upstairs to her room and lies in bed thinking how much things have changed in Mount Salus and in
this house. Now she hears the cars on the superhighway; as a
child she often went to sleep aware of the voices of her parents reading to each other. She finally is "sent to sleep under a
velvety cloak of words, richly patterned and stitched with
gold, straight out of a fairy tale" (58). Her last clear thought
before sleep overtakes her is that though she and Fay are sleeping much farther apart tonight than they did at the Hibiscus,
they are also much nearer. For Fay is sleeping in the bed where
she was born and where her mother died. She is so disoriented
in the once familiar but now strange environment that like
most moderns Laurel can discover no meaningful relationship to her past, or for that matter to the essence of human
mortality. Things were one way once, and they remained as
they were for a long time, but now they are all different.

3

The next morning when the participants in the "pageant of
grief" begin to arrive, it soon becomes apparent that what
is to occur on this day is almost a parody of the dignified
and solemn ceremony that Ransom had attributed to a traditional society. (Without the dogma the ritual slips away,

too?) Among the first guests to arrive are Fay's nonexistent family who have driven all the way from Madrid, Texas, (*Madrid* they pronounce to rhyme with *Mildred*) and they expect to drive back as soon as the funeral is over. (That the brother lives in a trailer and is in the wrecking business is significant in this context.) Inside the pickup truck and in the flat body behind the cab, they have brought Fay's mother, her brother Bubba (who wore a windbreaker, hardly the dress for a formal ceremonious occasion), her sister Sis, her nephew Wendell, and Sis's whole brood. The Chisoms, the mother says, are a close family: "Yes, me and my brood believes in clustering as close as we can get. . . . Bubba pulled his trailer right up in my yard when he married and Irma can string her clothesline as far out as she pleases. Sis got married and didn't even try to move away. Duffy just snuggled in" (70). (Is this the close family relationship that Davidson refers to?)

The mayor assures Laurel that everything the community can do to show its respect to its favorite son has been done— "bank's closed, most of the Square's agreed to close for the hour of services, county offices closed. Courthouse has lowered its flag out front, school's letting out early" (69). Laurel thinks, nevertheless, that nothing is going right. In the first place the nephew, Wendell, dressed in a cowboy suit with two holstered pistols, is enjoying his first funeral. All the Chisoms go by to look at the corpse—Laurel had wanted the casket to remain closed—and Bubba observes "he's young looking for a man pushing seventy-one." Mrs. Chisom reminds him that the reason *his* father had looked so "wasted" was that he "couldn't keep a thing down but tap water." " 'I'm proud of you, Wanda Fay,' " Mrs. Chisom says, "addressing the ceiling over her head." Even the old Chisom grandfather has come by bus from Bigbee, Mississippi, after having had to sit up all night waiting for the bus that reached the crossroads near his house at 3 A.M. He has spent his time on the bus hulling pecans, which he immediately gives to Laurel, saying, "Young lady, I carried you some Bigbee pecans. I thought you might not harvest their like here. They're last year's." Mrs. Chisom leads him up to the casket and asks him: "Out of curiosity, who does he remind you of?" The old man reflects for a moment and says, "Nobody" (77).

At the appropriate moment Fay bursts into the room, glistening in black satin. She looks neither to the right nor to the left; her eyes are fixed on the coffin. "Stop her," Laurel yells. "She's wasting no time, she's fixing to break aloose right now," Mrs. Chisom says. "Didn't even stop to speak to me." Sis steps in Fay's path and says, "Here I am Wanda Fay. Cry on me." "Get back," Fay screams, "who told them to come?" She rushes to the coffin, leans over it and coos, "Oh, hon, get up, get up out of there" (85). Laurel yells again, "Stop her." But Fay's performance is just beginning: "Can't you hear me, hon?" she calls. ("She's cracking," Mrs. Chisom says, "just like me. Poor little Wanda Fay.") "Oh, Judge, how could you be so unfair to me?" Fay yells. "Oh, Judge how could you go off and leave me this way? Why did you want to treat me so unfair?" Mrs. Chisom says Judge McKelva should have lived because Wanda Fay needed him. Even though he was a care and took all of your time, Mrs. Chisom asks Fay, pulling herself to her feet, "You'd take him back if you could have him, wouldn't you?" Fay cries into the coffin, "Judge, you cheated on me" (85). (Laurel will later recall her mother used almost the same words just before she died.) Then, fighting off Major Bullock, Mr. Pitts, her mother, and the preacher, Fay throws "herself forward across the coffin onto the pillow, driving her lips without aim against the face under hers. She was dragged into the library, screaming, by Miss Tennyson Bullock, out of sight behind the bank of greenery. Judge McKelva's smoking chair lay behind them overturned" (86). Mrs. Chisom's voice comes through the confusion of the library: "Like mother, like daughter. Though when I had to give up her dad, they couldn't hold me half so easy. I tore up the whole house, I did." Then Wendell draws one of his cap pistols and promises Fay to "shoot the bad man if you don't cry" (86). Surely Fay has her own idea of the part she should play in this "pageant of grief." As the grieving widow, she is the star of the show and, as such, she thinks she must give her audience a convincing performance. She must persuade the other mourners that no widow ever grieved as this one is grieving; and the more dramatic and outrageous the display, the more convincing will be the performance.

The funeral of Judge McKelva is attended by the entire community, religious or not, even though the pageant of grief is not exactly "lovingly staged." Major Bullock, the chief mourner, like Uncle Maury in *The Sound and the Fury* at Mr. Compson's funeral, makes too many visits to the sideboard and is completely intoxicated before the funeral begins. The members of the bar come as a group and station themselves together, out of sight, beyond the screen of ferns. There they converse among themselves on whatever topics they think of, as they light cigars in honor of the occasion. Becky's garden club is there, as are Laurel's six bridesmaids. The gathering crowd is joined by "a big apple-cheeked woman in a hairy tam" who enters the room majestically exclaiming, "I remember, Oh, I remember how many Christmases I was among those present in this dear old home in all its hospitality." After some difficulty, Laurel finally identifies this strange woman as Miss Verna Longmeier, whose only visits to the McKelva home were to sew in the little room upstairs. No one ever dared contradict Miss Longmeier, Laurel recalls, for if "a crooked piece of stitching were pointed out to her, she was apt to return: 'Let him who is without sin cast the first stone.'" The crowd, which by now has overrun the house and half filled the yard—where the Chisom children, who did not want to "view the remains," are picking the silver bells—is joined by Miss Thelma Frierson, who sold hunting and fishing licenses in the courthouse and who struggles to come up with "something good to say about the deceased" but can only mutter, "He had a wonderful sense of humor underneath it all." ("Underneath it all," Laurel says to herself, "Father knew it *wasn't* funny.") The mourners are joined by a "large, very clean man with rotund, open eyes like a statue," who Laurel knows, has "never been in the house but once before and that time he had come to tune the piano." He is Tom Farris, Mount Salus' blind man, who entertains himself by attending all the funerals in town.

While they are waiting for the services to begin—the Presbyterian minister, his wife says, is still at home struggling, attempting to find appropriate words "to do justice to Judge McKelva's memory"—almost everyone thinks of a story to tell. Although many of the tales are in some way related to Judge McKelva ("'Oh, I've modeled myself on this noble Roman,'" the mayor says dropping into his oratorical voice, "'and when I reach higher office . . . .'"), some of them are not. Bubba says doctors don't know how to do anything but charge, and Mrs. Chisom warms up by saying that she would not trust nurses for a "blessed second behind my back," before giving a vividly detailed account of how her son Roscoe committed suicide. Dr. Woodson tells how he saved the judge's life by carrying him a mile on his back after he cut his foot on a piece of rusty tin. Between visits to the sideboard Major Bullock tells how Judge McKelva had stood off a group of white caps who had come to town fully armed and determined to rescue a member of their group whom the judge had sentenced to be executed for premeditated murder.

As these stories become more and more astounding, Laurel's dormant emotions are aroused. She realizes they are talking about a man she has never known. When Major Bullock finishes his story, Laurel complains to Tish: "He is trying to make Father into something he wanted to be himself." Tish responds, "Bless his heart . . . . Don't spoil it for Daddy." But Laurel protests, "I don't think it's fair now." When Major

Bullock, finishing on a high note, declares, "Oh, under that cloak of modesty he wore"—Laurel protests, "Father was not modest"—but Major Bullock responds, "Honey, what do you mean? Honey, you were away. You were sitting up there in Chicago, drawing pictures" (80). (Finally, Laurel concludes, the only person she has ever known who would have done the things attributed to her father was her mother: "She's the only one I know who had it in her.") Her frustration grows as she listens to the stories: "They're misrepresenting him —falsifying, that's what mother would call it. . . . He never would have stood for lies being told about him. Not at any time. Not ever" (83). Miss Adele Courtland, to whom Laurel is speaking beneath the rumble of sound in the room, responds just as quietly: "Yes, he would . . . . If the truth might hurt the wrong person." But Laurel protests, "I'm his daughter. I want what people say now to be the truth. . . . The least anybody can do for him is *remember* right." That Laurel is unaware of the intentions of the "community of mourners" becomes increasingly clear.

The Mount Salus Presbyterian Church, which had been built by the McKelvas, is filled for the service, with the overflow, black and white, lining the walls and standing at the windows outside. After the service, little of which Laurel hears and what she does hear reminds her of the judge's table blessing, the procession moves to the cemetery where the top of the hill is "crowded with winged angels and life-sized effigies of bygone citizens in old fashioned dress, standing . . . like a familiar set of passengers collected on deck of a ship, on which they all knew each other—bona-fide members of a small local excursion, embarked on a voyage that is always returning in dreams" (89). (This reflection does not come from one who believes the destiny of the dead souls is Heaven. Immortality is a dream. Or perhaps, as Lacy Buchan says, death is merely a part of life.) This is the spot where all the McKelvas are buried, and Laurel naturally thinks her father will be placed among his kin. Fay has other ideas—"How could the biggest fool think I was going to bury my husband with his old wife?"— so they streak out across the field toward the new part of the cemetery, where there are already a few dozen graves "dotted uniformly with indestructible plastic Christmas poinsettias."

Everyone has come from the house to the church to the cemetery—Miss Tennyson Bullock is directing traffic, trying to get everyone, including blind Tom Farris, appropriately placed—the crowd, Laurel notes, even includes a few new groups. Miss Tennyson calls Laurel's attention to the high school band: "Look behind you. The high school band. They better be here! Clint gave 'em those horns they're sporting, gave 'em the uniforms to march in. Somebody pass 'em the word to perk up. Of *course* they're not going to get to play" (91). Then, the minister says a few words, trying to compete with the noise from the interstate highway, and Laurel knows the service is over, for the minister is passing down the line shaking hands with the family. Immediately behind the Reverend Dr. Bolt comes Dot Daggett, exclaiming, "I want to tell you, Laurel, what a beautiful funeral it was . . . . I saw everybody I know and everybody I used to know. It was old Mount Salus personified" (92). After the minister has said a few last words of comfort to the family, "the members of the high school band . . . are the first to break loose." They run toward their waiting jalopy, followed by Wendell, his holsters flopping against his legs, until he finds his pickup, climbs into the back and flings himself down on the floor.

After the funeral everyone gathers back at the McKelva house, where Bubba, while stuffing himself with the abundant food provided by the neighbors, observes to Fay, "Wanda Fay, you got enough stuff in sight to last one woman forever." Her mother adds that Wanda Fay had "done fine so far," that she was "proud of her" that day because the coffin was so attractive that she wished she "could have taken it right away from him and given it to Roscoe." Sis contributes her opinion:

that Fay "drew a good crowd too . . . without having to count those negroes." Mrs. Chisom can't imagine what use Fay will have for all the space in this huge house and suggests, "It'd make a good boarding house," if she could get her mother to come "to do the cooking for the boarders" (92–96). Suddenly Fay decides she will get in the pickup and ride with her family back to Texas.

While the reader is becoming thoroughly acquainted with the code of values under which the Chisoms operate, the narrator has apparently lost sight of Laurel. But the reader is aware of her presence and can well imagine the effect of these blatantly materialistic observations on this sensitive and deeply troubled young woman. (Fay has already let everyone know that the house is now hers and has broadly hinted that Laurel no longer is welcome there.) When Fay goes upstairs to pack, Laurel follows her to inform her of her travel plans in order to assure Fay that she will be out of the house before she returns from Texas. Then, unable to contain her curiosity any longer, she asks Fay why she had lied about not having a family. "It's better than some lies I've heard around here," Fay cries. As the pickup moves away from the house on its return to Texas, after dropping the grandfather at the bus station, Laurel can see Wendell standing in the back of the truck aiming his cap pistol and yelling, "Pow! Pow! Pow!" (100). Soon the others leave and Laurel is in the house alone.

4

The day after the funeral Laurel is working in the yard while three of her neighbors and life-long friends sit on the porch and review the events of the past few days. No one can believe that Fay will stay in Mount Salus, now that she can no longer "parade under the colors" of being Judge McKelva's wife. There are some half-hearted attempts to explain Fay's actions at the funeral. "You can't curb a Baptist," Mrs. Pease says, "Let them in and you can't keep 'em down when somebody dies." Then Miss Adele adds that she thinks Fay's bizarre behavior was just her idea of "giving a sad occasion its due . . . . She wanted nothing but the best for her husband's funeral, only the best casket, the most choice cemetery lot"— Miss Tennyson breaks in to remind her that the lot was not too choice, being so close to the highway, "not a thing Dr. Bolt was saying could be heard"—then Miss Adele continues: "the most brokenhearted, the most distraught behavior she could manage on the part of the widow." She even believes Fay was trying to raise herself in the estimation of the residents of Mount Salus, not realizing that the cultivated inhabitants of this traditional town would consider her behavior less than civilized, that Fay was completely misinterpreting their reason for being at her home before and after the funeral. So that the mourners not be obliged to run and throw themselves "upon the body in an ecstasy of grief," to use Ransom's words again, the mourners were there to provide an outlet for their sorrow through a "lovingly staged pageant of grief."

Then, half playfully, Miss Tennyson suggests that Laurel has no reason to return to Chicago, that she should remain to help the community keep Fay under control and to take Becky's place in what was once the best bridge foursome in Mount Salus. Only now do several divergent strains come together and all of them seem to indicate how certain forces once drew the residents of Mount Salus into a tightly knit community. Laurel's misunderstanding of the "pageant of grief" that was occurring at her father's funeral is almost as bad as Fay's. She does not realize that "the funeral in the most profound sense," as Cleanth Brooks points out, is "a social occasion of the highest order." As the members of the community gather around the bier to honor their most distinguished member, they reminisce, intending to fix in their memories an image of their friend a little bigger than life. But Laurel can only feel resentment because the views of her father they are presenting differ from the one she wants to preserve. She flatly accuses them of lying, with no realization of their intentions in slightly embellishing the facts.

The truth is that Laurel is no longer a member of the community of Mount Salus. "Of *course* she can give up Mount Salus," Miss Tennyson Bullock remarks, "and say goodbye to this house and to us, and the past, and go on back to Chicago day after tomorrow flying a jet. And take up one more time where she left off" (113). It is true, of course, that there is little to keep her in Mount Salus. With her father and mother both dead, she has no family ties in the community. The members of her husband's family, if there are any still living, undoubtedly reside, as he did, somewhere in the Midwest. She has not communicated with any of them since the funeral. There seems no real closeness among the six women who served as Laurel's bridesmaids. They seem to be trying to revive a closeness that once existed as they rally around Laurel in her time of sorrow, but there seems little day-by-day communication among them. Laurel is leaving, therefore, because she has no real ties in Mount Salus. She severed her connections with her community when she went to Chicago to study design, a profession she could not practice in Mount Salus; and she married a young architect from Ohio. (This disintegration is further suggested by the fact that "while the bridesmaids' parents still live within a few blocks of the McKelva house, the bridesmaids and their husbands had mostly all built new houses in the 'new part' of Mount Salus. Their own children were farther away still, off in college.") What we discover, then, is that not only has Laurel long ago cut the ties that bound her to home and community, but the community itself is disappearing; therefore Judge McKelva's funeral is a hollow and grotesque imitation of a "pageant of grief . . . lovingly staged and attended by a religious community."[4]

On her last evening in Mount Salus Laurel is left alone in

4 *Ibid.*, 35.

the house which was once her home, but which she realizes she can now inhabit only as a visitor; and with the relationship that exists between Fay and her, she knows it is highly unlikely she will ever "visit" it again. She is spending her last night in her home. If earlier in the story, the image of the fixed, seemingly unmoving, seagull has suggested the state of her numbed feelings as she brought her father's body home, the events of the last few days, and her realization that she has only a final night to discover some acceptable relationship with her past, have deeply disturbed her. Now not the hanging, motionless seagull but the chimney swift—a prisoner in the house, forever moving, darting from the lower floor to the top of the house, going from one room to another, movement without meaning or direction—suggests her innermost feelings. If the chimney swift is intended to suggest the turbulent state of Laurel's emotions, as I believe it does, one can see that she, too, is like the man at the gate of the Confederate cemetery in the "Ode to the Confederate Dead." She is cut off from the traditions of her society. Her life is moving toward no specific objective because she is living in a purposeless world. She must discover the true nature of the past that lies behind her personal past, which she has never really paused to consider, and one which, as Miss Tennyson Bullock says, she is attempting to blot out completely.

As she contemplates her past, she finds that everything does not fit the neat pattern she has formed in her mind. First, she tries to determine her exact feelings toward Fay, what their future relationship will be. "It was not punishment she wanted" to give her, she tells herself, but she craves "acknowledgment"—"admission that she knew what she had done" (131). At the same time she realizes that Fay was not really aware of what she had done. "Fay," Laurel understands, was only making a little scene—"that was all. . . . Death in its reality passed her right over." Death as the ultimate act of existence did not escape Becky's notice, but almost to the end of his life this realization had evaded the Judge, who prided himself on his optimism. Then Laurel wonders if she is "as lost a soul" as Fay is because she cannot feel pity for her, as her father did; or pretend to feel it, as the citizens of Mount Salus do. Although her father when he came to realize the reality of death did not imitate her mother's conduct, Laurel realizes she is following Fay's. "What would I not do, perpetrate," she wonders, "for consolation?" Her feelings, she realizes, are finally personal, selfish; she wants to be consoled for the loss of her parents and to receive public acceptance of her attitude toward Fay.

Her desire to solidify the image she retains of her mother, her realization that she can tell no one how she feels toward Fay, how miserable the judge's second marriage really was, leads her to search the house for some concrete irrefutable evidence to support her illusion of her parents' almost perfect marriage. Her conviction that the union between the judge and Becky was ideal is suggested by her memory of the many nights she went to sleep listening to their "loving voices" reading to each other. The home they created together, her memory tells her, was the one of "firelight and warmth." As she sits in the little sewing room, which had once been her bedroom, she remembers the roaring fires her father had built, and she feels the spiritual warmth of belonging somewhere, to someplace when she sees the "1817" carved into the side of her mother's secretary, which had been made from cherry trees grown on the McKelva farm.

Looking through the relics of her life in this house—as her memory is savored with the pleasure she associates with her own brief marriage, which has contributed greatly to her image of an idyllic past—she discovers that her memory is not flawless; some facts are not as she remembers them. Some things of the past have slipped slightly out of kilter, just as Fay has changed some of the furniture in the rooms. Only after searching for some letters from her mother to her father does she recall that he saved no letters from anyone. He answered them immediately and destroyed them. Although her mother saved and carefully filed all of the letters she received from her husband, Laurel discovers with a discomforting jolt, after reading the letters and thinking about her parents' life together, that their marriage was not completely happy. Her mother was never a member of the Mount Salus community; home to her was the house atop the mountain in West Virginia in which she grew up. Laurel recalls the stories her mother told her, demonstrating the closeness of that family —her father and mother, her six brothers and herself. Her mother's story of her heroic journey down a raging river to get her ill father to a doctor convinces Laurel that in West Virginia her mother was "too happy to know what went on in the outside world." In Mississippi her mother was a displaced person, as rootless as Fay is, and, Laurel soon realizes, as she herself is. Once when her mother returned to Mount Salus, with memories of her parents' home fresh in her mind, Becky said scornfully, "Where do they get the *Mount*? There's no mount here." Laurel suddenly realizes that when she cuts her final tie to the community in which she was born and raised, she is losing her self-identity. In Chicago she will be an anyone living anywhere; she might as well be returning to New York or Los Angeles.

Laurel remembers that during her mother's last illness she had for a time turned against Judge McKelva because he could do little for her; "he was not passionately enough grieved at the changes in her." He could not believe, Laurel decides, that all of his wife's difficulties would not turn out all right, that she was going to die, "because there was nothing he would not have given her." Almost with her dying breath her mother had exclaimed, "Why did I marry a coward?" Although her father had tried to convince his wife that everything would be all right, she had responded, "I've heard that before." For the first time Laurel realizes her mother regarded her father as a coward because he would not accept death as the ultimate reality. For this reason we can understand the nature of Judge McKelva's optimism and comprehend a little what must have been occupying his mind during his last days. Laurel, we recall, comes into his room just before his death, and suspects by the appearance of his arm that he is no longer concentrating. What conclusion has he reached concerning his own death? He has come to accept his own mortality as he never could his wife's.

The realization, finally, that her parents' marriage lacked something essential, especially when her mother needed her father most, convinces Laurel that she has idealized her past, that like most moderns, in Allen Tate's term, she is a new provincial, a prisoner of the present moment. As Miss Welty points out in "Some Notes on Time in Fiction": "What can a character come to know of himself and others by working through a given situation? This is what fiction asks, with an emotional urgency driving it all the way; and can he know it in time?" [5] Laurel's deeply disturbing realization that her parents' life together, especially in her mother's final years, was most difficult because her father would not accept human mortality leads her to reexamine her own marriage, which she has always felt was unblemished. But now since she is looking critically at the past for the first time, her husband, Phil, "looked at her out of eyes wild with the craving for his unlived life, with mouth open like a funnel's." She knows that her life with Phil, because it was so brief, was basically unfulfilled, and "she wept for what had happened to life." For the first time she realizes how badly he hated to give up life when he had barely begun to live. She wonders if, through withdrawing, she is not refusing to accept life. She is making little effort to select the experiences that will be her life, a choice no one else has. Why is she choosing to lose herself in Chi-

5 Welty, *The Eye of the Story*, 166.

cago? Does she really have a choice? These are the kinds of questions she asks herself.

This night of introspection and soul searching starts "the deepest spring in her heart to flowing again." One final scene with Fay lets her understand without question which of her past experiences—all of which had tended to degenerate into rosy, abstract feelings of peace and security—she can carry with her back to Chicago. After a thorough search, trying to dredge up some concrete moments of her past happiness in this house, she comes upon the breadboard which her husband Phil had made for her mother. Her mother had always cherished the board, kept it cleaned and polished, and Laurel was convinced that the quality of Becky's bread was improved because it was made on this board. This breadboard will be a constant reminder to her, she believes, of her existence in things tangible, an object which her dear husband constructed with loving care and which her mother cherished. It becomes for her, in Ransom's terms, a "precious object," an "aesthetic form." Just as she discovers that the board is now scarred and discolored because Fay has used it to crack black walnuts on, Fay unexpectedly returns from Texas. So profound is Laurel's sorrow at the appearance of the board that she shows it to Fay and says, "You have desecrated this house." Fay responds in characteristic manner that she doesn't know what the word means but that she does know this house and everything in it, including the breadboard, belongs to her. Laurel is able, then, after days of self-torture, to bring the disparate elements of her experience—man's mortality, her father's two marriages, her own, her own unexamined view of the past—into focus: Experience finally does assume its right order, "which is not always the order of other people's time." She realizes that "Fay was Becky's own dread." That her mother knew Fay was coming was one of the reasons that she feared death, feeling that in her husband's attempt to replace her she would be betrayed. When Fay says that Laurel is not going to scare her into leaving Mount Salus, Laurel asks "What were you trying to scare Father into—when you struck him?" "I was trying to scare him into living!" Fay responds. This response is another way of saying that she, like Becky, is merely trying to force him to realize his deepest human feelings.

Laurel returns to discussing the breadboard, saying, Phil "loved good bread." And Fay responds, "What's he got to do with it? He's dead, isn't he?" With the conviction that her feeling for Fay is as real as that for her dead father, mother, and husband, "For there is hate as well as love,"—and both are human emotions and a basic ingredient of life—Laurel comes to a final evaluation of Fay, who "was without any powers of passion or imagination in herself and had no way to see it or reach it in any other person." As Fay has said, "the past isn't a thing to me. I belong to the future." But Laurel now knows since Fay is oblivious of the past, the future is impervious to her. What Laurel has discovered about her past— though it is quite different from what she had supposed it was —is removed from Fay's influence, but she has discovered Fay's basic humanity. She is also a true modern, she is really bound by traditional values little more than Fay is, she can leave her home—the sense of community as a specific place evoking definite emotional reactions has long been absent from her feelings toward Mount Salus. She can return to Chicago, chastened by the realization that she is her father's daughter, as useless to him in his time of need as he was in his first wife's. But she has profited from the events of the past few weeks; she can experience genuine emotion again. She realizes that no amount of wishful nostalgic longing can make the past much different from the present, for the past, as Faulkner once said, "is not dead, it is not even past." The past is time, however, and how one experiences time is his only means of affecting his own mortality. What Laurel learns, finally, is that it is impossible to place human relationships into one neatly labeled compartment and expect it to remain there quietly and unchanging forever. Not only is it unlikely that one human being will know another, but the quality of their relationships is forever changing.

VI Redeeming Grace: Flannery O'Connor's The Complete Stories

One of the convictions held by the twelve southerners who contributed to *I'll Take My Stand: The South and the Agrarian Tradition* (1930) was that man is a fallible finite creature, and that any society created by him would contain the imperfections of its creators. Another of the principles upon which all members of that symposium agreed was that religion cannot be expected to play a vital role in a modern industrial society. A vast difference existed among the several contributors concerning the particular function of religion in modern society. In "Religion and the Old South," Allen Tate argues that Protestantism, a creed which, as Ralph Gabriel has pointed out, emphasized the individual and his emotions and a "gospel of love which cleanses the world," is designed to support an aggressive, materialistic urban society. Such a religion, Tate insists, undermines the basic Christian myth which should be in "conviction immediate, direct, overwhelming."[1] The modern tendency toward positivism and scientific abstraction has destroyed the myth on which Christianity depended for existence.

John Crowe Ransom shared many of Tate's concerns, but Ransom's suggestions

1 Allen Tate, "Remarks on the Southern Religion," in *I'll Take My Stand* (Baton Rouge: Louisiana State University Press, 1977), 156.

for man's actions in the face of the continual encroachments of reason and science upon religious faith were often quite different. He agrees with Tate that modern man has abused "the best of his myths." Since Ransom believes religion is essential to man's happiness on any plane of existence, he emphasizes that man should attempt to restore the myth by which he could know an inscrutable God. The function of religion in the post scientific world in which man now lives is the point at which Ransom's thinking differs from Tate's. His position is near that of Jed Tewksbury, the protagonist of Robert Penn Warren's *A Place to Come To* (1977), who asserts that to ask man to accept the dogma of organized religion is "to fly in the face of the whole intellectual history of the western world since the Renaissance." Ransom proclaims, therefore, in his *The World's Body* (1938) that "religion is an institution existing for the sake of its ritual, rather than, as I have heard, for the sake of its doctrines." For the rituals of religion are, Ransom asserts, one of the important characteristics of a civilized society, and the best religious thinkers of the day realize that the "issues upon which doctrines pronounce" may be addressed only through aesthetics. When an issue which doctrine addresses presses itself on man, he had best not attempt to understand "the precise event but enlarge its terms" and try to assimilate it into the "form of an ornate public ritual." Man's personal faith will not enable him to meet the crises and calamities of this life, or the most emotionally laden experience of all—his awareness of the awesome certainty of death, of his own death or that of a loved one. If he is going to avoid what Allen Tate calls the abyss or if he is to prevent his falling into the malaise, the modern sickness of unbelief, Ransom insists that man brought up on scientific fact must depend upon the customs, orders, rites and ceremonies of a civilized society—decisions slowly arrived at over the past several centuries.

In *All the King's Men*, as we have seen, Jack Burden had

to acquire a metaphysic that justified the existence of evil in the universe and assigned man's responsibility for the results of personal action before he could unify the disparate elements in his personality. The nature of his belief was not highly orthodox, including, as it did, Ransom's God of Thunder, the God of omnipotence, if not of wrath, of the Old Testament, but omitting entirely any reference to the New Testament God of faith, from which man could acquire the strength and the wisdom to confront the soul-destroying problems of modern living. Allen Tate and Eudora Welty suggest the possibility that civilizing ritual cannot continue to exist apart from dogma.

Flannery O'Connor, however, is one of the few significant writers who lived and wrote in the South between 1925 and 1965 who accepted unquestioningly the dogma of the church of which she was a devout member. She believed, as she said in the words of Pascal, "'in the God of Abraham, Isaac, and Jacob and not of the philosophers and scholars.' This is an unlimited God and one who has revealed himself specifically. It is one who became man and rose from the dead. It is one who confounds the senses and the sensibilities." She believed in this God, although she realized that it was a "stumbling block," and that there was "no way to make it more acceptable to modern thought." This God, she concludes, was the effect of her "ultimate concern and he has a name." Man, O'Connor argues in another essay, lost his "innocence in the Fall" and the only means by which he can be returned to it is "through the Redemption which is brought about by Christ's death and by our slow participation in it." Modern man's greatest flaw is that he has reduced his "conception of the supernatural to pious cliches." [2] "When they ask you to make Christianity look desirable," she wrote Sister Mariella Gable, "they are asking you to describe its essence, not what you see.

2 Flannery O'Connor, *Mystery and Manners* (New York: Farrar, Straus, and Giroux, 1969), 161, 148.

Ideal Christianity doesn't exist, because anything the human being touches, even Christian truth, he deforms slightly in his own image. Even the Saints do this. I take it to be the effects of Original Sin."[3]

This orthodox Christian view is at the heart of O'Connor's fiction; certainly it is its primary concern. So central is the Christian theme to O'Connor's stories and novels that it could be argued that she is not really a southern writer at all. Eudora Welty has explained the function of place in fiction. "Place in fiction," she writes, "is the named, identified, concrete, exact, and exacting, and therefore credible, gathering spot of all that has been felt, is about to be experienced, in the novel's progress. Location pertains to feeling; feeling profoundly pertains to place; place in history partakes of feeling, as feeling about history partakes of place."[4] If the function of literature, as Ransom insists, is the reconstitution of experience, its nature is profoundly affected by an individual's attitude toward a specific concrete place. How much a literary creation can be charged by an individualized character's attachment to a well-delineated unique place can be observed when John Barth creates its opposite, an alienated contemporary man with no location, an anyone living anywhere.

Many of O'Connor's stories are set in Georgia, and few writers have had a better ear for southern speech or a more accurate knowledge of southern idiom. Mrs. Pritchard, a character from "A Circle in the Fire," comes over to her landlady's house one morning "sour-humored, because she had nothing calamitous to report," and complains "'I got the misery in my face today' . . . holding on to what she could salvage. 'Theseyer teeth. They feel like an individual boil.'" (191). The young mother in "A Good Man Is Hard to Find" has a face "as broad and innocent as a cabbage," and her daughter,

June Starr, says her grandmother would not have missed their vacation trip "to be queen for a day." The grandmother has dressed carefully so that if they have an accident, "anyone seeing her dead on the highway . . . will know at once that she was a lady" (118).[5] Later when the grandmother has led them on a foolish search for a nonexistent house and the cat she secretly brought along causes an accident, she remains "curled up under the dashboard" while the children, June Starr and her brother, scramble out of the car and begin yelling, "We've had an ACCIDENT!" She hopes that her son's wrath will not "come down on her all at once. The horrible thought she had had before the accident was that the house she had remembered so vividly was not in Georgia but in Tennessee." When she emerges from the car, she comes pressing her side and exclaiming, "I believe I have injured an organ" (125).

Despite her uncanny ability to reproduce the eccentricities of southern speech and her profound knowledge of southern character and temperament, these and the other technical accomplishments in O'Connor's fiction—the broad humor, the biting irony, the enviable ability to underscore human fallibility through the use of carefully selected detail—are secondary to its Christian theme. Her characters often appear only incidentally as southerners. Primarily they are men and women who are involved in the universal struggle between good and evil. There is no indication that the place of their birth, and the one in which they have always lived, is "the gathering spot of all that has been felt, is about to be experienced." Her stories are not didactic, but they are concerned with man's attitude toward his condition. Once when she was asked why some of her characters are strange, grotesque, a little freakish, she responded: "When you can assume that your audi-

---

5 Flannery O'Connor, *The Complete Stories* (New York: Farrar, Straus, and Giroux, 1971), 191. All references are to this edition, and page numbers will be given in the text.

ence holds the same beliefs you do, you can relax a little and use normal means of talking to it; when you have to assume that it does not, then you have to make your vision apparent by shock—to the hard of hearing you shout, and for the almost blind you draw large and startling figures." O'Connor's conviction that man's journey through the world is a perilous venture is ample justification, she believes, for the use of such startling language and so many grotesque figures. To support her case, she quotes Saint Cyril of Jerusalem: "The dragon sits by the side of the road, watching those who pass. Beware lest he devour you. We go to the Father of Souls, but it is necessary to pass by the dragon." [6]

Like that of Eliot and Tate, the past that O'Connor was able to retain was the continuing tradition of orthodox Christianity. The world that she attempts to delineate in her fiction emphasizes the varied forms the dragon may take as man makes his necessary passage by him. In story after story, therefore, she focuses our attention on one aspect or another of her view of metaphysical reality. She explains to one of her correspondents why she believes her stories, though firmly grounded in orthodox Christian theology, can cover a broad range: "I guess what you say about suffering being a shared experience with Christ is true, but then it should be true of every experience that is not sinful. I mean to say, joy, may be a redemptive experience itself and not just the fruit of one. Perhaps however joy is the outgrowth of suffering in a special way." [7] To another, she gives further explanation of why so many apparently fanatic Protestants appear in her books. The first reason is her conviction that the writer should call up the "general and maybe the essential through the particular." She lives in a section, she points out, in which Protestants predominate; therefore most of her characters are Protestant. But

6 O'Connor, *Mystery and Manners*, 34, 35.
7 Fitzgerald (ed.), *Letters*, 527.

why are there so many Protestant fanatics? Her answer to this question is equally clear and convincing:

> People make a judgment of fanaticism by what they are themselves. To a lot of Protestants I know, monks and nuns are fanatics, none greater. And to a lot of monks and nuns I know, my Protestant prophets are fanatics. For my part, I think the only difference between them is that if you are a Catholic and have this intensity of belief you join the convent and are heard from no more; whereas if you are a Protestant and have it there is no convent for you to join and you go about the world getting into all sorts of trouble and drawing the wrath of people who don't believe anything much at all down on your head.[8]

In *All the King's Men* Jack Burden insists at one point that man may view the past only in one of two ways, either cynically or sentimentally. O'Connor's "Good Country People" dissects an old pious stereotype to demonstrate that sentimentality, which would include Burden's view of nostalgia, is merely "an excess, distortion of sentiment usually in the direction of innocence." Hulga Hopewell, a thirty-year-old atheist with a Ph.D. in philosophy, sets out to seduce a nineteen-year-old Bible salesman, whom her mother has described as "just good country people . . . the salt of the earth." After the Bible salesman has called on her mother and stayed for dinner—through which Hulga ignores him, not even responding to his questions—Hulga walks with him to the gate and, surprisingly, arranges for an assignation the next day at ten. During the night she imagines that she seduces him: "that the two of them walked on the place until they came to the storage barn beyond the two back fields and there, she imagined, that things came to such a pass that she very easily seduced him and that then, of course, she had to reckon with his remorse. True genius can get an idea across even to an inferior mind. She imagined that she took his remorse in hand and changed it into a deeper understanding of life. She took all his shame

8 *Ibid.*, 517.

away and turned it into something useful" (284). She is going to relieve him of his superstitious view of the relationship between the physical and metaphysical realms and introduce him to a rational view of reality. She would show him, she is convinced, that "I'm saved and you are damned" because "I don't believe in God." She has no illusions; she is "one of those people who see *through* to nothing" (287).

The next day they meet at the appointed time, and the encounter seems at first to follow much easier than she had expected the pattern she had set for it. They walk across the field to the barn and enter the loft; then the boy begins "methodically kissing her face, making little noises like a fish." At first she does not return any of the kisses, but after a while "she reached his lips and remained there, kissing him again as if she were trying to draw all the breath out of him" (287). She has seduced him, she thinks, without even trying; she "decided for the first time in her life she was face to face with real innocence" (289).

She is surprised, at the height of her amorous conquest, when he asks to see "where her wooden leg joins on," for "she was as sensitive about the artificial leg as a peacock about his tail" (288). After a moment, in which she feels "as if her heart had stopped and left her mind to pump her blood," she replies, "All right"; it was as if she had surrendered to him completely, as if she had lost her life and found it again, "miraculously, in his" (289). When she tries to get him to put her leg back on, he put it in his valise, along with the "hollowed-out Bible containing a small flask of whiskey, a pack of cards with obscene pictures on them, and a box of contraceptives." When she asks if he is not "good country people," the "perfect Christian," he responds: "I hope you don't think . . . that I believe in that crap! I may sell Bibles but I know which end is up and I wasn't born yesterday and I know where I am going!" As he left her, helpless without her wooden leg, he says, "And

I'll tell you another thing, Hulga . . . you ain't so smart. I been believing in nothing ever since I was born" (291).

As Flannery O'Connor has pointed out, the wooden leg accumulates meaning as the story progresses.[9] We know that Hulga is a spiritual as well as a physical cripple, that she believes in nothing, and that the wooden leg corresponds to that part of her soul that is wooden. When the Bible salesman takes her wooden leg, she realizes her incompleteness for the first time. This is the moment of awareness that comes, as O'Connor has pointed out, to almost all of the major characters in her stories. To most of them, since they like all men have fallen and are therefore sinful, she offers salvation. But some are unaware of the fateful moment they are experiencing, are insensitive to God's grace, and substitute some form of secular enlightenment for it. Such has been Hulga's solution to the problems that have confronted her, and this story ends before we can be certain that her mind-boggling experience with the Bible salesman has changed her fundamental concept of the nature of the world in which she lives.

Although some of Miss O'Connor's characters don't have the slightest inclination toward the religious point of view— George F. Rayber in *The Violent Bear It Away*, Shepherd in "The Lame Shall Enter First"—some are aware of religious values but fail to act on their belief. Mrs. McIntyre, of "The Displaced Person," has a strong sense of what is right, she is industrious and frugal, and she has an acute realization of her community responsibilities. She gives a Polish refugee, Mr. Guizac, and his family a place on her farm, and although the Pole quickly establishes himself as the best worker she has ever had, she watches silently as his body is crushed beneath the wheels of a tractor. Her hatred of Mr. Guizac is the result of his having proposed a scheme to free his niece, an in-

9 O'Connor, *Mystery and Manners*, 99.

nocent child of sixteen, from a camp for displaced persons—both her parents have died in similar camps—by marrying her to Sulk, a hand on the place, whom Mrs. McIntyre describes as a "thieving, halfwitted, black, stinking nigger." So great is Mrs. McIntyre's prejudice that she is unable to realize that Mr. Guizac is merely using the marriage as a means of rescuing his niece from the indignities and tortures of the camp. After Mr. Guizac's death, her life completely disintegrates: her hired hands leave, her well-kept farm is neglected, and Mrs. McIntyre is hospitalized with a nervous affliction—all the apparent result of her refusal to accept grace when it is offered.

On one occasion O'Connor referred to the positive effect on her art of her belief in Christianity. "Actually," she wrote, "it frees the story teller to observe. It is not a set of rules which fixes what he sees in the world. It affects his writing primarily by guaranteeing his respect for mystery." [10] Although almost any of her stories show her "respect for mystery," the point is emphatically demonstrated, I think, in "A Temple of the Holy Ghost." Two young girls, both fourteen and both students at Mount Saint Scholastica, come from the convent to spend the weekend with their cousin and her twelve-year-old daughter. All weekend the two girls—Susan, with a "pretty pointed face and red hair," and Joanne, with "yellow hair that was naturally curly"—kept calling each other Temple One and Temple Two. The two girls are obsessed with their emerging sexuality and begin every sentence with, "You know this boy I know well one time. . . ." When their hostess asks why they refer to each other in such a strange manner, they respond, often interrupting themselves in fits of giggles, that Sister Perpetua, the oldest nun in the convent, "had given them a lecture on what they should do if a young man should . . . 'behave in an ungentlemanly manner with them in the back of

10 *Ibid.*, 31.

an automobile.'" They were to inform the young gentleman, in Sister Perpetua's words: "'Stop Sir! I am a Temple of the Holy Ghost!'" (238).

Seeking some kind of entertainment for the two girls over the long weekend, the hostess follows her daughter's suggestion and invites Wendell and Cory Wilkins, two young apprentice Church of God ministers, to come to supper and take Susan and Joanne to the fair. The young men come and before supper sit with the two girls on the porch. "They sat like monkeys," O'Connor reports, "their knees on a level with their shoulders, and their arms hanging down between." They have brought a harmonica and a guitar and soon they begin to play and sing a song that sounded "half like a love song and half like a hymn." The two girls mock the boys by singing a hymn from the benediction. The boys, who have had no experience with Catholicism, think "that must be Jew singing" (241).

After dinner the boys take the girls to the fair, where the main attraction is a freak with a name they can't remember:

> The tent where it was had been divided into two parts by a black curtain, one side for men and one for women. The freak went from one side to the other, talking first to the men and then to the women. . . . The freak had a country voice, slow and nasal and neither high nor low, just flat. "God made me this way and if you laugh He may strike you the same way. This is the way He wanted me to be and I aint disputing His way. I'm showing you because I got to make the best of it. I expect you to act like ladies and gentlemen. I never done it to myself nor had a thing to do with it but I'm making the best of it." (245)

When the two girls return from the fair, they tell their hostess' daughter what they have seen, and she lies in bed trying to visualize the effect the freak's revelation had on the audience:

> She was better able to see the faces of the country people watching, the men more solemn than they were in church, and the women stern and polite, with painted-looking eyes, standing as if they were waiting for

the first note of the piano to begin the hymn. She could hear the freak saying, "God made me this way and I don't dispute it. . . . Raise yourself up. A temple of the Holy Ghost. You! You are God's temple, don't you know? Don't you know? God's spirit has a dwelling in you, don't you know?"

"Amen. Amen."

"If anybody desecrates the temple of God, God will bring him to ruin, and if you laugh, He may strike you this way. A temple of God is a holy Thing. Amen. Amen."

"I am a temple of the Holy Ghost."

"Amen." (246)

The next afternoon the two girls are driven back to the convent by Alonzo Myers, an eighteen-year-old boy who works for the taxi company, weighs two hundred and fifty pounds, and smells so bad the windows of the taxi have to be kept open. The twelve-year-old daughter sits on the front seat with Alonzo and her mother in the back with Joanne and Susan. When they arrive at the convent, they are informed that benediction is just beginning. "You put your foot in the door," the daughter thinks, "and they get you to praying." The child kneels by her mother, and they "were well into '*Tantum Ergo* before her ugly thoughts stopped and she began to realize that she was in the presence of God" (247). She begins to pray silently. On the journey home, the child and her mother learn from Alonzo that some of the preachers from town had had the fair closed down because of the sideshow in which the freak displayed its hermaphroditic body. The child looks across a stretch of pasture land and observes the setting sun, "a huge red ball like an elevated Host drenched in blood and when it sank out of sight it left a line in the sky like a red clay road hanging over the trees" (248).

This scene presents explicitly that "moment in every great story in which the presence of grace can be felt." It comes, obviously, as the child participates in the benediction service at the convent. In the middle of that service, as she becomes increasingly aware of her own religious significance, she realizes the real meaning of the hermaphrodite's spiel: man's body, even *his* despite its corruption and grotesqueness, is really the dwelling place of God. The creature's speech is delivered as a litany, to which the audience responds "Amen." On the ride home Alonzo Meyers is not thought of as fat and repulsive. The principal thrust of this story is well summarized by Professor Carter Martin: "The conclusion of the story makes specific the mysterious identity of man's body with God's being by presenting through the child's mind the convergence of the body of Christ, as the Host in the Catholic service of benediction, and the body of the hermaphrodite."[11] As O'Connor says, "When your audience is hard of hearing, sometimes you have to shout."

Not only do some of her characters reject grace when it is offered; some, like Harry Ashfield's parents in "The River," remain unaware of their human potential. The story opens with the parents, who have celebrated too vigorously the evening before, trying to rid themselves of their four-to-five year-old boy for the day so that they can recuperate. The sitter who has come at six A.M. to collect him and take him to her home for the day—she really intends to have him hear a faith-healing preacher perform—complains of the foul odor of cigarette butts and half-consumed drinks in the apartment. The father grumpily tries to get them out the front door so that he can get back to bed.

Later that day the boy hears the Reverend Mr. Bevel Summers proclaim: "There ain't but one river and that's the River of Life, made out of Jesus' Blood. That's the river you have to lay your pain in, in the River of Faith" (165). Then the boy tells Mrs. Connin that his name is Bevel and that he has never been baptized. When she reveals this fact to Mr. Summers, he says, "Swang him over here." She passes the boy to Mr. Summers who is standing in the edge of the river. Just before the

11 Carter Martin, *The True Country: Themes in the Fiction of Flannery O'Connor* (Nashville: Vanderbilt University Press, 1970), 111.

boy is plunged under the muddy water, "He had the sudden feeling that this was not a joke. Where he lived everything was a joke" (167). The preacher tells him, "If I baptize you . . . you'll be able to go to the Kingdom of Christ. . . . Do you want that?" After he has baptized the boy, he tells him, "You can count now. . . . You didn't count before" (168).

When Mrs. Connin and the boy get back to the apartment in the late afternoon, another party is in progress. Mrs. Connin sees Harry's mother, in "long black satin britches and barefoot sandals and red toenails" lying on the couch. She doesn't get up until Mrs. Connin tells her that Harry has been baptized and that the preacher, who is a healer, "prayed for you to be healed." "Healed!" the mother shouted, "Healed of what for Christ's sake?"

"'Of your affliction,' Mrs. Connin said icily." Of course the woman has no notion of what her affliction is, so the remark means nothing to her. The father responds flippantly, indicating the shallow depth of his awareness, "Go on, go on. . . . I want to hear more about her affliction. The exact nature of it has escaped . . . ." (169). The mother asks Harry what the preacher said, and he responds: "He said I'm not the same now . . . I count." She pauses just a moment, almost as if she is pondering the significance of that remark, then "she lowered him by the shirt front onto the pillow." (The moment in which grace is offered to her passes unheeded.) She hangs over him an instant and brushes her lips against his forehead. Then she gets up and moves away, "swaying her hips lightly through the shaft of light" (171). The juxtaposition of the sensual phrase "swaying her hips lightly" and "through the shaft of light" suggests that O'Connor is reminding us of the woman's spiritual blindness, that she is oblivious to the "presence of grace" to which she has been subjected.

The next morning Harry arises before his parents, eats "two crackers spread with anchovy paste," and drinks some stale ginger ale from one of the bottles left on the coffee table.

Then he finds "some raisin bread heels" and spreads a "half jar of peanut butter between them." When he finishes, he finds some chocolate milk, drinks that, decides his parents "will be out cold until one o'clock," wanders about the room emptying full ashtrays on the floor, and feels his shoes still damp from the river the day before: "Very slowly, his expression changed as if he were seeing appear what he didn't know he had been looking for. Then all of a sudden he knew what he wanted to do" (172). He gets up, tiptoes out of the room and heads for the river. He walks into the water, puts his head under and begins to gasp, he tries again and decides the "River of Faith" won't have him: "He gave one low cry of pain and indignation. . . . He plunged under once and this time the waiting current caught him like a long gentle hand and pulled him swiftly forward and down. For an instant he was overcome with surprise: then since he was moving quickly and knew he was getting somewhere, all his fury and fear left him" (173–74). His spiritual longing to rejoin the living Christ overcomes the physical desire for self-preservation in a scene so vividly presented that even the almost blind cannot fail to perceive it.

Some of O'Connor's characters live in a state of almost perpetual grace, like Lucynell Crater, the thirty-year-old deaf mute with poor eyesight in "The Life You Save May be Your Own." These are nature's innocents whose rational faculties do not allow them to choose between good and evil; therefore they live peacefully under the influence of God's all-embracing love. Mrs. Turpin's vision in "Revelation" reveals the great variety of beings encompassed by God's redeeming grace:

> There was only a purple streak in the sky, cutting through a field of crimson and leading, like an extension of the highway, into the descending dusk. She raised her hands from the side of the [pig] pen in a gesture hieratic and profound. A visionary light settled in her eyes. She saw the streak as a vast swinging bridge extending upward from the earth through a field of living fire. Upon it a vast horde of souls

were rumbling toward heaven. There were whole companies of white-trash, clean for the first time in their lives, and bands of black niggers in white robes, and battalions of freaks and lunatics shouting and clapping and leaping like frogs. And bringing up the end of the procession was a tribe of people whom she recognized at once as those who, like herself and Claud [her husband] had always had a little of everything and the God-given wit to use it right. (508)

Some of her characters, like the grandmother in "A Good Man is Hard to Find," come to know God for the first time: The Misfit's voice "seemed about to crack and the grandmother's head cleared for an instant. She saw the man's face twisted close to her own as if he were going to cry and she murmured, 'Why you're one of my babies. You're one of my own children!' She reached out and touched him on the shoulder. The Misfit sprang back as if a snake had bitten him and shot her three times through the chest" (132). The grandmother is left half-sitting and half-lying "in a puddle of blood with her legs crossed under her like a child's and her face smiling up at the cloudless sky." O'Connor's statement of her intention in the story is instructive:

> I often ask myself what makes a story work, and what makes it hold up as a story, and I have decided that it is probably some action, some gesture of a character that is unlike any other in the story.
>
> . . . .
>
> There is a point in this story where such a gesture occurs. The grandmother is at last alone, facing the Misfit. Her head clears for an instant and she realizes, even in her limited way, that she is responsible for the man before her and joined to him by ties of kinship which have their roots deep within the mystery she has been prattling about so far. And at this point, she does the right thing, she makes the right gesture.[12]

For her pains, of course, she gets three bullets in her chest, and the Misfit says: "She would of been a good woman . . . if it had been somebody there to shoot her every minute of her life." O'Connor's discussion of the Misfit's function in the

12 O'Connor, *Mystery and Manners*, 111–12.

story is also interesting: "I don't want to equate the Misfit with the devil. I prefer to think that, however unlikely this may seem, the old lady's gesture, like the mustard-seed, will grow to be a great crow-filled tree in the Misfit's heart, and will be enough of a pain to him there to turn him into the prophet he was meant to become." [13]

Some of O'Connor's characters—like Mrs. Cope of "The Circle in the Fire," who pulls weeds and nutgrass out of her flower beds "as if they were an evil sent directly by the devil to destroy the place"—are so selfish in their attachment to their material possessions that they are unable to achieve their full human potential. "Think of all we have, Lord," she sighs early in the story, as she looks around at her "rich pastures and hills heavy with timber; we have everything." When she thinks of those "poor Europeans" whom "they put in boxcars like cattle" and cart off to Siberia, she thinks she ought to spend half of her time "on her knees."

Her complacency is soon disturbed, however, and her selfishness and hypocrisy revealed. Powell Boyd, whose father once worked for Mrs. Cope, and two of his friends, Garfield Smith and W. T. Harper, come down from a low-income housing development in Atlanta, where they all now live, to have a vacation in the country. For months, one of the boys says, Powell has "been telling us about this here place. Said it was everything here. Said it was horses here. Said he had the best time of his entire life right here on this here place. Talks about it all the time" (180). It soon becomes obvious that the plight of these three boys is just as desperate as that of the "poor Europeans," but the Europeans represent an abstract condition that Mrs. Cope does not have to confront in the flesh, so she can easily feel sorry for them. She is a true modern who can deal successfully with a set of circumstances that she can reduce to an abstraction, but the three boys are con-

13 *Ibid.*, 113.

crete particularities, and they are a threat to that which belongs to her. Although they live in a concrete jungle in which they can tell their home from the other houses like it only by its smell, and although it is apparent that Powell has used the farm as a means of escape from the sordidness of his home environment, Mrs. Cope's selfishness will permit her to assist him in no way. One of the boys says: "He ain't ever satisfied with where he's at except this place here. Lemme tell you what he'll do lady. We'll be playing ball see, on this here place in this development we got to play ball on, see, and he'll quit playing and say, 'Goddam, it was a horse down there name Gene and if I had him here I'd bust this concrete to hell riding him!" (182). But Mrs. Cope can only scold him for his use of profanity and tell the boys they cannot ride the horses because she "was afraid someone would get hurt on her place and sue her for everything she had."

The boys decide that Mrs. Cope doesn't "own them woods. . . . Gawd owns them woods and her too"; therefore they remain on the place, ride the horses, cavort in the woods, and enjoy their stay in the country. Several times Mrs. Cope tries to get them off her place, but all of her efforts are unsuccessful. Once at sunset, her concern becomes obsessive, and the sun seems to be burning so fast that it is "trying to set everything on fire." Even after Mrs. Cope has threatened to call the sheriff if they don't leave, her daughter, listening to a shriek in the dark, does not share her mother's belief that the boys are gone. The next morning, therefore, the child goes into the woods, trying to find them. She sees them standing by a watering trough and hears one of them say to Powell, "If this place was not here any more . . . you would never have to think of it again" (192). Then they engage in a kind of ritualistic chase through the woods, after which they "began to set the brush on fire. They start to whoop and holler and beat their hand over their mouth and in a few seconds there was a narrow line of fire between her and them" (193). Mrs. Cope immediately spots the blaze and gets her hired hands to try to put out the fire, but they have little effect on it. The daughter looks into her mother's face and sees an expression there she has never seen before: "The child turned her head quickly, and past the Negroes' ambling figures she could see the column of smoke rising and widening unchecked inside the granite line of trees. She stood taut, listening, and could just catch in the distance a few wild high shrieks of joy as if the prophets were dancing in the fiery furnace, in the circle the angel had cleared for them" (193). This figure, included in the last sentence in the story, brings to an arresting climax its many religious images and implications and makes with clarity and emphasis the principal point, especially to those readers who know the scriptural passage upon which this final image is based.

Of all important southern writers of the period under consideration, Flannery O'Connor is the only one whose religious orthodoxy becomes the central thesis in her fiction. William Faulkner apparently was not an orthodox Christian; at any rate his interest in religion, as far as his fiction is concerned, was, like Ransom's, in its ritual, not in its dogma. Although Tate's announced interest in Catholicism reaches at least as far back as 1930, he employs Christian imagery in his fiction primarily to demonstrate its importance as a ritual deeply affecting the actions of his characters. In some of his poetry, however, Christianity appears as an all-consuming faith that can transform the nature of the world in which we live. Although in much of Warren's fiction the quest of the protagonist to recover his traditional past appears an almost obsessive motif, the search never concludes in a manner acceptable to the orthodox Christian. To do so, as Jed Tewksbury says, would attempt to refute all intellectual history since the Renaissance. The nature of Warren's fictional characters' never-ceasing search appears clearer in some of his poetry, as in *Eleven Poems on the Same Theme* (1944), in which the protagonist seems to be seeking his irrational self and the relationship between it and Jung's "Collective Unconsciousness." Walker Percy, it is true, is Catholic, but the elements of his faith are never used in a direct and undisguised form to present the crucial issues in his novels. Like John Barth's early fiction, Percy's characters are struggling with nihilism and trying to find some acceptable relationship to the indifferent world in which they must live. In her undeviating attention to the essence of her beliefs, Flannery O'Connor sometimes appears almost as "strange and freakish" as some of the characters she creates, but her unwavering attention to the dragon that sits with insatiable appetite by the side of the road over which we all must pass has given us some of the most impressive, interesting, and enlightening fictional situations in modern American literature.

VII Intimations of Mortality: Walker Percy's The Moviegoer

One of the basic differences between the modern southern writer, one of the generation of Faulkner and Tate, and the contemporary writer, one whose best work was done after World War II, is their different attitudes toward the nature and use of the past. The writer in the period between the two wars was attempting to establish, as Lewis P. Simpson points out, a significant and usable relation to the past. The contemporary southern writer, like his counterparts elsewhere, is not primarily concerned with "the restoration of a civilization"; instead he is involved in the "intensely personal struggle" of attempting "to find some meaning in an absurd and undefinable world." [1] A close reading of Walker Percy's *The Moviegoer* (1961) is, I think, one certain means of proving the validity of Simpson's thesis.

One night Binx Bolling, a young stockbroker from New Orleans who is the protagonist of Percy's novel, awakes on the porch of his mother and stepfather's fishing camp near Biloxi. After an outing with his secretary, Sharon, at Ship Island and a movie at a drive-in theater with her and some of his stepbrothers and sisters, Binx has slept soundly for a few hours. Then for

[1] Lewis P. Simpson, *The Dispossessed Garden* (Athens: University of Georgia Press, 1975), 90.

no apparent reason he suddenly awakens. All he knows is that he is wide awake, a fully formed concept filling his mind. Neither his mother's family—after his father is killed in World War II his mother has married Roy Smith, a Western Auto dealer in Biloxi and has six children—nor his father's family —composed now of his Great-Aunt Emily and her husband Jules Cutrer, in whose home he has grown up—understands how he is trying to conduct his life, the nature of what he calls his "Search." His mother's family, he says, thinks he has lost his faith and prays for him to recover it. As far as he is concerned, however, he doesn't know what they are talking about, because, as he admits, "I could never make heads nor tails of God. The proofs of God's existence may have been true for all I know, but it didn't make the slightest bit of difference. . . . In fact I have only to hear the word God and a curtain comes down in my head." His father's family, particularly his Great-Aunt Emily, believes that the "world makes sense without God and anyone but an idiot knows what the good life is and anyone but a scoundrel can live it." [2]

Here, then, in his own family Binx has represented the two views of the past that lay behind much of the writing produced in the South between the two wars, the Christian concept of the temporal and transcendent view of history, a belief in a God-centered universe that has operated as a moving force in Western European civilization for two thousand years, and the classic stoical view that a man should not expect much from a world from which the gods have disappeared. He does have, the holders of this view insist, the ritual and ceremony, even though he can no longer embrace the dogma of religion, so that a "certain manner and a certain grace" can guide man at the most trying moments of life—"success, failure, marriage and death" (222). This philosophy is just as incomprehensible to Binx as the Christian view. These two conflicting

2 Walker Percy, *The Moviegoer* (New York: Noonday Press, 1961), 146. All references are to this edition, and page numbers will be given in the text.

ideologies pulling with equal force in opposite directions render Binx impotent. All he can do, he says is lie in a semicomatose state completely submerged in everydayness, the malaise he has been trying to fight off for the past eight years by the search in which he is engaged. Finally his muscles relax so that he can get up and write in his notebook:

REMEMBER TOMORROW
Starting point for search:
It no longer avails to start with creatures and prove God.
Yet it is impossible to rule God out.
The only possible starting point: the strange fact of one's own irreducible apathy—that if the proofs were proved and God presented himself, nothing would be changed. Here is the strangest fact of all.
Abraham saw signs of God and believed. Now the only sign is that all the signs in the world make no difference. Is this God's ironic revenge? But I am onto him. (146)

In an attempt to establish an acceptable relationship between himself and an undefinable and apparently indifferent universe, Binx sets out to follow the systematic approach suggested by Kierkegaard's religious existentialism. Percy describes Binx's search in terms of Kierkegaard's designation of the modes of human existence—aesthetic, ethical and religious—and in all significant aspects Percy's employment of these philosophic descriptions of the levels of existence available to man follows closely those advanced by Kierkegaard. Long before the publication of *The Moviegoer*, in an essay entitled "The Man on the Train," and elsewhere, Percy had demonstrated his mastery of Kierkegaard's theories. In *The Moviegoer*, however, he uses Kierkegaardian philosophy primarily to provide structure and a definite body of substance to Binx's search. He is writing a novel, not a philosophical treatise; therefore he is attempting to reconstitute human experience, not to make some comment about it. Binx's struggle to find himself, therefore, is composed primarily of two parts. First, he must establish that he is "someone living somewhere," not "anyone living anywhere." This feat he attempts to accomplish by becoming fully aware of the concrete particularities of the physical world around him—its distinctive sounds and odors—and to become thoroughly acquainted with his sensual self. By manipulating experience and by employing what Kierkegaard called "rotation" and "repetition," Binx was able to accomplish this first objective, but of far more importance, as far as the dramatic conflict of this novel is concerned, is a second objective, that of establishing his position in what once seemed to him a meaningless universe. He is able to accomplish this objective by experiencing two profoundly stimulating human experiences—his sincere compassion for his half-brother Lonnie, including his discovery of a means of feeling genuine satisfaction when Lonnie escapes human suffering through death, and his growing awareness that his feeling toward Kate Cutrer is that of human love. These two experiences, in Kierkegaardian terms, allow Binx to experience "intersubjectivity" so that through "the leap of faith" he can move into the religious mode of human existence. To understand Binx's movement through the Kierkegaardian modes of human existence, it would be helpful, I think, to present the details of his experience more or less in the order that they occur to him, even to the point of violating slightly the sequence in which they are presented in the novel itself.

2

Binx had become aware of the possibility of a search eight years before in Korea, where he lay wounded in a ditch—a bullet fragment "nicked the apex of my pleura and got me a collapsed lung and a big roaring empyema"—and watched an "oriental finch scratching around in the leaves" (206). Then he saw plain for the first time. It was the only time, he says, when the grip of everydayness had not dominated his life, and he vowed he would not be defeated by the modern malaise.

When he returned home, therefore, he set out with two friends to do some hiking. They began at Gatlinburg and headed for Maine up the Appalachian Trail. Drinking and talking about physical love, poetry, and Eastern religion seemed like great fun for a while, but soon Binx got depressed. When they did have fun, "like sitting around a fire or having a time with some girls," it seemed to him that it was all staged, as if they were trying too hard to amuse themselves. So Binx, sunk "in a deep melancholy," realized no matter how much they deserved to be happy nor how badly he wanted to make them so, he simply could not (41). He left them, therefore, and went back to New Orleans, where he finally wound up in Gentilly. He swore he would never attempt to have friends again. From that time to this, he says, he has lived in constant wonder.

Binx does not forsake the "search," however, and he undertakes a program of reading "fundamental books," books on key subjects:

> Such as *War and Peace*, the novel of novels; *A Study of History*, the solution of the problem of time; Schroedinger's *What Is Life?*, Einstein's *The Universe as I See It* and such. During those years I stood outside the universe and sought to understand it. I lived in my room as an Anyone living Anywhere. . . . Certainly it did not matter to me where I was when I read such a book as *The Expanding Universe*. The greatest success of this enterprise, which I call my vertical search, came one night when I sat in a hotel room in Birmingham and read a book called *The Chemistry of Life*. When I finished it, it seemed to me that the main goals of my search were reached or were in principle reachable. . . . The only difficulty was that though the universe had been disposed of, I myself was left over.[3] (69–70)

Binx realizes, then, that he is on the wrong kind of search. What he finds in the books he reads is not important. What is important is what he finds as he wanders about the neighbor-

---

3 In *The Message in the Bottle* (New York: Farrar, Straus, and Giroux, 1975) Percy refers to Kierkegaard's "little Herr Professor who fits the entire world into a scientific system but does not realize that he himself is left out in the cold and cannot be accounted for as an individual."

hood.[4] After a brief stay in the "old world atmosphere" of the French Quarter—he already knows the "genteel charm" of the "garden district," where he grew up—he moves to Gentilly and settles in an apartment in the basement of Mrs. Schexnaydre's home.[5] There is, Percy points out, a kind of "conscious parallel between Binx going to Gentilly and Phillip going to the Gaza Desert. . . . Gentilly is a desert if ever there was one." Binx, then, in Percy's view of man is a "pilgrim in transit, in journey," and since he is on Kierkegaard's aesthetic level, he is "consciously cultivating certain experiences . . . living in a certain place with a certain feeling to it and having sensations about being there."[6] In his frontispiece Percy quotes from Kierkegaard's *The Sickness unto Death* on the nature of despair: "The specific character of despair is precisely this: it is unaware of being in despair." Binx is trying very hard to avoid the depth of despair, the unrelenting grip of everydayness, by manipulating his experiences as best he can. First of all he is a model citizen and takes great pleasure in doing what's expected of him. He has a wallet full of identity cards, library cards, and credit cards. He has a small strong box in which he keeps his personal papers: his discharge from the army, his insurance policy, his birth certificate, and the deed to a "defunct duck club" in St. Bernard Parish. It is as if his individuality, his peace of mind, and even his right to exist

4 Since science cannot say "one single sentence about what a man is himself as an individual," the person who accepts the scientific view of reality has a limited perspective "in which he sees the world ordered in scientific constructions with himself as a great lacuna." John Carr (ed.), *Kite-flying and Other Irrational Acts*, (Baton Rouge: Louisiana State University Press, 1972), 39. I doubt that Percy read Ransom's criticism, but this statement is near Ransom's assertion that science gives a distorted and limited view of reality because it attempts not "to reconstruct reality" but to make "some abstract statement about it."

5 "Binx lived almost entirely," Percy says, "in what Kierkegaard calls the aesthetic mode" (*Kite-Flying*, 49). It is appropriate, therefore, that he live in a basement, as it is that his step-cousin Kate, who lives in the same mode, spends most of her time preparing a TV room for her father in the basement of their home.

6 *Ibid.*, 48, 49.

are certified by the neat styrene cards he carries around in his pocket.

He lives a quiet life in Gentilly. (In the garden district he was always dissatisfied with the state of things, and he oscillated between writing letters to the editor trying to bring about change and lapsing into a state of depression and lying as "rigid as a stick" when he knows he can do nothing.) He manages a branch of his uncle's brokerage firm, spends his evenings watching television or going to the movies, and on weekends he has a fling with his secretary of the moment on the Mississippi Gulf Coast. Many of the points of exaltation in his life, as he tries to manipulate his sensory experiences, come not from actual experiences but from the movies— when the cat finds Orson Welles in the doorway or when John Wayne shoots down three men in the street with his carbine. His visits to the coast are exciting, for he gets sensual stimulation from pursuing one of his beautiful secretaries and is able to avoid temporarily the spiritual agony of becoming completely submerged in everydayness. When the secretary succumbs, however, the situation changes. She usually allows him to seduce her because she thinks sexual intercourse is an expression of love which will lead to marriage. Love—like manners, rites, ritual, custom, and God—is a word which Binx "can't make heads or tails of," and every time he contemplates it, he goes plunging to the depth of despair, completely caught up in the malaise. He has to indulge in a minor kind of rotation. Although at this period of his life Binx is living on the edge of everydayness, he never completely becomes engulfed in its identity-destroying fog. Binx, as Percy has pointed out, consciously cultivates "living in a certain place with a certain feeling to it, and having sensations about being there." [7] Every evening as he walks across to the paro-

7 *Ibid.*, 49.

chial school to sit on a bench and look through the papers for the movie schedules, and then to get a bus and ride ten miles into Algiers, he is very much aware of what he is doing. It is a consciously planned, highly individualized experience. He is definitely someone, living somewhere, and doing something he has decided he wants to do. He notes, however, that the school is a model of American efficiency, and he feels a deep sense of security because he owns a few shares of Alcoa, and the school is constructed of aluminum.

Although Binx comes dangerously close to the brink of the abyss, he never falls in, and one morning he gets that "quincy queazy" taste of 1951 and Korea. It is not fear but the smell of fear. He is reminded of the first time the possibility of the search occurred to him, and he realizes he has almost forgotten. He is flirting with disaster because he has become almost oblivious to being in despair. But this morning he became aware of the items that go in his pocket, each as a separate concrete object: wallet, notebook, pencil, keys, handkerchief, slide rule. He is aware for the first time they are his and for that reason are unlike similar objects existing elsewhere in the world. Furthermore because he owns these specific items in this particular combination, he is different from all other people. He is someone living somewhere. Because he is aware of these objects in their concrete particularities, he is again convinced of the possibility of the search. He carefully bathes, shaves, and dresses; then he sits down at his desk and pokes through the pile. He is like the castaway on the island searching for clues of where he is and how he got there or like "the detective on television . . . searching through the dead man's possessions, using his pencil as a poker" (11).

On the morning he becomes aware again of the possibilities of a search, he is invited to lunch by his aunt. He knows that something unusual might happen, for today is Wednesday and he always has dinner with her on Sunday. Either she is going to talk to him about her stepdaughter Kate, or she is going to have one of her serious talks with him about his future. He doesn't find the prospect unpleasant because he knows that something out of the ordinary is going to occur, a development that he always finds promising and stimulating. The idea of the search comes to him again as he rides the street-car to his aunt's. (He owns a car but he seldom uses it because he thinks it makes him invisible. As they cross the street, peo-ple look not at him but at his left rear fender to see if he is out of their way.) On the streetcar he sees an attractive young girl and thinks how things would be different if this were a movie. He could speak to her, they could become acquainted, and maybe they could go off to the coast. This is reality, however, and the moment of separation will soon come. He thinks again of the search and is convinced that it is what everyone would be involved in if he were not sunk in the everydayness of his own life. "This morning," he thinks as he recalls the incident of his becoming really aware for the first time of the contents of his pockets, "I felt as if I had come upon myself on a strange island. And what does such a castaway do? Why he pokes around the neighborhood and he doesn't miss a trick. . . . To become aware of the possibility of the search is to be onto something. Not to be onto something is to be in despair" (13) Movies, he thinks, are onto the search but they always screw it up; they end in despair. Although they present a heightened view of reality, they always leave their characters sunk in everydayness. He asks himself, a searcher, what do you seek? Is it God? A recent poll, he recalls, shows that 98 percent of the people believe in God and 2 percent don't. Everyone, it would seem, is satisfied with what he has, and that doesn't leave much room for a searcher. Like Kierkegaard's little pro-fessor, he is left over. He doesn't even know how he stands, if he is ahead or behind his fellow Americans. Have all the others found what they want or are they so bound up in everyday-ness that the possibility of a search never occurs to them?

He alights in the French Quarter, so acutely aware of his

surroundings that it is almost as if the raw ends of his nerves are exposed. He smells the roasting coffee and wet creosote. He sees the iron railings (they "sag like rotten lace") and the "sweating carriage ways." Then he sees William Holden (he knows that Holden is making a movie in the area and he has stopped with the hope of seeing him) and a young honey-mooning couple. The young groom has fallen into every-dayness; the honeymoon has not been as interesting or as stimulating as he had expected. This day, which should be a highlight of his life, is too much like all other days. His bride knows something is wrong with him, although she doesn't know what; his mood affects her and she, too, sinks into every-dayness. Just when their day seems spent, Holden asks some ladies from Hattiesburg for a light for his cigarette. They lose their composure at seeing him, and the young boy, noncha-lantly, without a hint of recognition, flicks his Zippo for Hol-den, and walks on, a different person. A minor rotation has occurred, something out of the ordinary has happened, and he walks along with a new spring in his step and a slight swagger. He puts his arm around his bride's shoulder, she senses his change of mood and nuzzles her head against his neck. For the moment they have been rescued from everydayness, and Binx moves on behind Holden, noting that as the movie star goes along "an aura of heightened reality moves with him and all who fall within it feel it" (16).

As he is savoring his astonishment at the ability of movie stars to rescue ordinary people from the pits of everydayness that they usually inhabit, he sees a parade passing and ob-serves that no one seems aware of it. He *sees* the people around him in a new perspective, against the background of an ap-proaching storm; they seem "tiny and archaic" and he *senses* that the "fog of uneasiness has settled on the street." Then he really *looks* at the passing parade and observes the legs of the girls on the float, one of whom he thinks is Linda, his former secretary, and he is amazed to realize that her legs, which he

has seen hundreds of times, are not as good as he had supposed them to be. After the parade passes Binx meets Eddie
Lovell, a successful lawyer and an old acquaintance who has
married Binx's cousin, a man so deeply and completely en-
grossed by the routines of his life—making money, rediscov-
ering himself by reading *The Prophet* aloud with his wife,
collecting antiques, being model husband, father, and a useful man in the community, speaking and thinking in the most
time-worn and meaningless stereotypes—that he epitomizes
one so submerged in everydayness that he is out of touch with
anything that really matters, one who is truly in despair because he is unaware of being in despair. Sometime later he
meets Eddie's wife Nell and she says she and Eddie have re-
viewed their values and found them "pretty damn enduring,"
that their only purpose in life is "to make a contribution, however small, and leaves the world just a little better off." Binx
can only think, "another forty years to go and dead, dead,
dead" (101–102). The last time Binx met Eddie he found his
eye closing in a big involuntary wink. Although the wink is
not a conscious action, it is not a twitch, as was that of Warren's old man at the gas station in Don Jon, New Mexico.
Binx's eye motion is almost an unconscious sign of his will's
saying, "Neither of us really believes that meaningless series
of sounds that you are mouthing, do we?"

When Binx arrives at his aunt's residence, he is met at the
door by Mercer, a black man whom Aunt Emily brought from
the family plantation into town when she married Jules Cutrer.
Mercer is a man of no fixed identity; it is almost as if he is
practicing the Mythotherapy prescribed for Jacob Horner in
John Barth's *The End of the Road*. To Aunt Emily he is loyal
retainer, butler, footman, and chauffeur. To himself he is a
cityman, well informed in economics, science, and politics, a
man of the world able to demonstrate his superiority to the
tradesmen with whom he conducts business by stealing from
his employer. But, as Binx notes, he is so busy shifting from

role to role that there is hardly any of *him* left. After Mercer has shown Binx inside to await the arrival of Aunt Emily, Binx's heightened awareness begins to see, really see, the Cutrer sitting room, which he has visited many times: "its walls of books, its bokhara glowing like a jewel, its blackening portraits. The prisms of the chandelier wink red in the firelight" (23). He looks at the pictures of his father and uncles on the mantel and, as he has so many times in the past, he can't get beyond the expression in his father's eyes, one that he can't identify. He cannot make his aunt's picture of a "student prince" fit the portrait of the "ironic dude on the mantel, with the fraternity blazer, the straw katy pushed back releasing a forelock." (He joined the RCAF in 1940 and was killed in Crete before America entered the war. "And in the wine dark sea with a copy of *The Shropshire Lad* in his pocket.") Again Binx searches his father's eyes, "each eye a stipple or two in a blurred oval. 'Beyond a doubt,' [he concludes,] 'they are ironical'" (25).

As Binx waits, he is looking forward to one of his aunt's attacks because it raises the day out of the ordinary, out of the muck of everydayness. When she comes, she begins by calling him "an ingrate, a limb of Satan, the last and sorriest scion of a noble stock," and he forgets all his years in Gentilly, even the search. Then she gets to the point of the unexpected luncheon invitation. Her stepdaughter Kate, who has emotional difficulties and is under the care of a psychiatrist, vows that she will not go to one of the Mardi Gras functions in which her fiancé Walter will participate. Too, Kate has been drinking and taking drugs—from fear of her approaching marriage her stepmother believes—and she wants Binx to talk to her.

Then his great-aunt begins her serious talk with him. She asks him what he wants out of life and tells him she wants him to enter medical school in the fall, that she has had an apartment prepared for him in her backyard. He tells her he doesn't know what he wants out of life but that he will move in whenever she wants him to. The means by which he earns his living seems of little importance to him. At best, it is peripheral to his primary interest. "Don't you want to make a contribution?" she asks, and he replies, "No'm" (54). She is exasperated, she says, because the things she once held sacred are "reviled and spat upon." She does not know the destiny of the universe; no gods, she tells Binx, have revealed any secrets to her, but one thing she does know: "A man must live by his lights and do what little he can and do it as best he can. In this world goodness is destined to be defeated. But a man must go down fighting. That is the victory. To do anything less is to be less than a man" (54).

This is the philosophy by which certain southerners have lived for more than a hundred years, and it is one that Bayard Sartoris and Lacy Buchan would understand perfectly, but Binx, though he agrees with his great-aunt, admits that nothing she says has any bearing on the problems that confront him. At the moment, however, even the *idea* of a search seems absurd to him. His heart sinks, moreover, when his aunt says that all young men must have their *Wanderjahr*. If what he has been doing for the past eight years is merely a *Wanderjahr* before "settling down," he concludes, he'll shoot himself (55).

After he has had his "serious talk" with his aunt, Binx finds Kate in the basement she is renovating for a television room for her father. That Binx is aware of her physically is indicated by his observation of her shapely derriere, but he is also concerned about her health. She is one of Percy's truly alienated characters. As Percy admits to John Carr, she "was on the point of blowing up in a thousand pieces all the time, suffering acute anxiety." [8] Robert Coles explains the precise nature of Kate's anxiety: "What has caused anxiety now becomes a refuge from it. That is, assumptions are turned around,

8 *Ibid.*, 47.

so that the alienated person almost welcomes disasters, unsettling surprises, even the possibility of an apocalyptic moment. Life as it is lived from day to day seems futile, purposeless, a tiring bore. . . . Habits once cheerfully followed now seem pointless. And worst of all, it seems to the alienated person, are those efforts on the part of the unalienated to 'interpret' alienation." [9] Kate deeply resents Aunt Emily's attributing her anxiety to "uneasiness about her approaching marriage" to Walter, a reaction which Emily insists is perfectly normal under the circumstances. Kate tells Binx the happiest moment of her life was a part of the catastrophe that resulted in the death of her fiancé, Lyell. They were coming back from a football game in Oxford. Near Port Gibson, Lyell passed a car, a coupe with "Spry painted on the door." "Spry was the last thing I saw," Kate says, "because Lyell ran into a truckload of cotton pickers." She was not seriously hurt in the accident, and when she went over to look at Lyell, everyone thought she was an onlooker. "When was the happiest moment?" Binx asks her. "It was on the bus," she responds: "I just stood there until the door opened, then I got on and went sailing along from bright sunshine down through deep clefts as cool and dark as a spring house" (59–60). After the bus has taken her into Natchez, she gets a hotel room, takes a bath, has her blouse cleaned, and takes the train home. Kate tells Binx that he is just like her—he's not, for he's not as disoriented as she —"You make mother believe you are a regular go-getter," she says, "but I know better. You are like me, only worse" (43). After their "little" talk, which Emily had arranged, Binx and Kate meet downtown, have some oysters, and see *Panic in the Streets* with Richard Widmark, a movie made in New Orleans. One scene is made in the very neighborhood in which the theater is located, and after the movie—they don't talk during movies in order not to break the spell of unreality, the

9 Robert Coles, "Walker Percy," *New Yorker*, October 2, 1978, p. 86.

release from everydayness—Kate says, "Now the neighborhood is certified." Binx explains her remark: "She refers to a phenomenon of moviegoing which I have called certification. Nowadays when a person lives somewhere, in a neighborhood, the place is not certified for him. More than likely he will live there sadly and the emptiness which is inside him will expand until it evacuates the entire neighborhood. But if he sees a movie which shows his very neighborhod, it becomes possible for him to live, for a time at least, as a person who is Somewhere and not Anywhere" (63). By her reference to certification, which she calls one of "your little researches," Binx realizes she is playing a role, losing the struggle to maintain her self-identity. She is trapping herself too often. When she breaks her engagement to Walter, her attitude worries Binx. Her family is too considerate, she insists, too understanding. She wishes they would kick her out of the house so that she could become an airline stewardess. Binx fears, however, that she is not merely seeking release from life's routines and duties but that subconsciously she is hoping for another ordeal, another life-destroying accident like the one that killed Lyell.

3

Since business is slow on the weekend before Mardi Gras, Binx carefully prepares Sharon, his present secretary, to get her in the mood to accompany him to the Mississippi Gulf Coast. Everything around him reminds him of the search and how badly it's going. Only a few hours alone with her in his MG, "leg to leg and haunch to haunch," and a romp on the sands of Ship Island, he decides, will push back the tide of everydayness that threatens to drown him. "Desire for her," he says, "is like a sorrow in my heart." After his careful planning to change the nature of their relationship from boss-secretary to woman-man—like Gregory Peck or Dana Andrews with movie heroines—he is not really surprised that they are suddenly on their way, "like two children lost in a summer afternoon who, hardly aware of each other, find a door in the wall and enter an enchanted garden" (106). At Bay St. Louis he has a nearly perfect "rotation," which gives him a chance to escape the malaise which threatens to destroy him, a whiff of which he caught as they came through the swamps of Chef Menteur, "a little tongue of hellfire" licking at their heels. The rotation, as Kierkegaard says in *Either/Or*, is a means by which we attempt to rid ourselves of "the ruinous character of boredom" by rotating our experiences. As he says: "One tires of the country and moves to the city, one tires of his native land" and moves away. Binx refines this definition. A rotation, he says, is "the experiencing of the new beyond the expectation of experiencing the new." He has entertained certain expectations of his trip to the coast—different scenery, new physical stimulations, particularly those associated with his new relationship with Sharon—but this trip exceeds those expectations. First, on the way down a green Ford rams into the side of the MG, and although the car is not badly damaged, Sharon is very solicitous and examines him closely to see if he is badly hurt, holds his head, examines an old war wound, and removes his shirt and undershirt. His excitement at their physical closeness and her deep and sincere concern is enough to rid him momentarily of the malaise. They go to Ship Island, swim, embrace, cavort on the beach, and generally enjoy each other's companionship. On the way home they pull into a bay, have a drink, and he is so happy that he decides, "It's not a bad thing to settle for the Little Way, not the big search for the big happiness but the sad little happiness of drinks and kisses, a good little car, and a warm deep thigh" (135–36). One might have to settle for a pure sensuous relationship, one unencumbered by any human emotion except physical desire and its gratification. After their drink they go down to Binx's mother's fishing camp and meet her new family, her husband Roy Smith and five of their six children. Duvall, the oldest, was drowned the previous summer. Lonnie, now the oldest, is crippled, confined to a wheelchair. He is Binx's favorite for he, too, is a moviegoer. "Like me," Binx says, "he will go to see anything. But we are good friends because he knows I do not feel sorry for him. For one thing, he has the gift of believing that he can offer his suffering in reparation for man's indifference to the pierced heart of Jesus Christ," a conviction that Flannery O'Connor would understand and respect. His mother, Binx notes, is deep within everydayness because "by the surest of instincts she steers clear of all that is exceptional or stimulating" (138).

Binx is disturbed by Lonnie's looks because he seems so thin, and he is appalled to learn that Lonnie is fasting to "conquer an habitual disposition." He envied Duvall, Lonnie says, while he lived and is glad he is dead. Lonnie is offering his communion for Binx, he says, because he loves him. Among the Smiths, all of whom are practicing Catholics, Lonnie is the only devout one. Binx and Lonnie enjoy the movie they see after dinner because of the little touches they share that no one else sees—in itself a very definite rotation—but on the way home the next day the little MG becomes infested with the malaise. Even when he reaches over and touches Sharon's thigh at its deepest part, he is not relieved. Physical desire, it would seem, is not always sufficient.

4

Soon after their return he learns that Kate has taken an overdose of sleeping pills. When he talks to her about it, she tells him she was not trying to commit suicide but merely to get off dead center. The experience has obviously provided her with an ordeal, almost as good as that of the accident, and she reports that she has had "one of the best nights of my life." She knows that Binx is going to Chicago on business for her father. She tells him that she wants to go with him and that they should leave that evening on the train.

On the train, shortly after leaving New Orleans, Binx experiences a "repetition" and his life becomes merely a sojourn between train rides. A "repetition" Percy defines as "the reenactment of past experience toward the end of isolating the time segment which has lapsed in order that it, the lapsed time, can be savored of itself and without the usual adulteration of events that clog time like peanuts in brittle" (79–80).[10] He gives other examples of repetition: fourteen years ago in the spring of the year he had gone to see *The Oxbow Incident*, and when he came out of the movie there was "the smell of privet . . . and the camphor berries popping underfoot." The details of that first experience are uncannily repeated. "There we sat, [he went with Kate, this time] I in the same seat, I think, and afterwards came out into the smell of privet. Camphor berries popped underneath on the same section of broken pavement" (79). On another occasion he picked up a German language newspaper and read in it an advertisement for Nivea Creme, "showing a woman with a grainy face turned up to the sun." He had read the same advertisement and seen the same picture of the same woman in the same paper twenty years before (80). "The events of the intervening twenty years were neutralized, the thirty million deaths, the countless torturings, uprootings, and wanderings to and fro." Nothing of any importance could have happened because there was the woman's picture unchanged by the ravages of time, like the engraven images on the Grecian urn. The "repetition," then, as a device to raise one immured in everydayness works actually opposite to the manner in which "rotation" functions. Rather than provoking stimulating sensory experiences to lift him from the duties and routines of life, one deliberately looks inward. There he stands, apparently oblivious to passing time, and he asks himself: What was I like back then? What was the texture of life? What are the forces that brought me from

10 Carr (ed.), *Kite-Flying*, 50.

then to now? A successful repetition arouses in man the passionate urge to explore his roots and character.

Just before they leave for Chicago, after Kate has made an unsuccessful attempt at apparent suicide, Aunt Emily calls Binx and reads him the latest entry in Kate's diary: "Tonight will tell the story—will the new freedom work—if not no more tight rope for me" (110). Kate has viewed the abyss yawning at her feet while she is under the stifling influence of the malaise, and she feels she is always straining at the leash that holds her back. Binx has concluded, as we have seen, that it is ordeal that Kate is seeking, and his concern is so unsettling that he cannot sleep—he never sleeps soundly—and he goes outside for a breath of air. Kate comes up in a taxi. She asks Binx if she can ruin her whole life with one act of which she is not aware. Binx notes that she is "taut as a bow string," all bound up with idea. He can see that she is all involved in what he calls "an exalted moment," that she expects to be transported by some traumatic happening into another realm of experience. He is wary, for he has long since abandoned the possibility of the vertical search. For the first time, she says, she is free because she doesn't have to be anything, not what her family wants, not what her doctor expects, nothing. (She is like Matthieu, a character in Sartre's *The Reprieve* who while walking on the Pont Neuf declares himself free because "within me there is nothing." Percy has responded to this argument, however, by saying that even to be *Nothing* is to be *Something*.) Until now, she says, she has been afraid to reveal that she is hiding nothing. Binx can see that she is struggling at her exaltation, so without any preliminaries he asks her to marry him. Kate responds that she is afraid and asks, "What am I to do?" "We'll get in my car," Binx says, "and go down to the French Market and get some coffee. Then we'll go home." "Is everything going to be all right?" she asks. "Yes," he says, "Everything's going to be all right."

Later, as they ride in the observation car toward Chicago, Binx is very much impressed with the manner in which a methodical well-organized young man is reading his newspaper. He folds it "into a neat packet exactly two columns wide," props it against his knee, and when he sees something that strikes him as important, he takes out a gold pencil and neatly encircles the item. Occasionally he takes a small pair of scissors from his pocket, clips a passage, folds it neatly, and places it in his wallet. As he sits there nodding, watching the man from St. Louis, he is aware that Kate is white and shaking beside him; his mind wonders to an autograph party given for Dr. and Mrs. Bob Dean, authors of a book called *Technique in Marriage*. As his eyelids droop, he imagines the Deans, a heavily freckled, oldish couple demonstrating their technique of lovemaking, all purely mechanical, all honest human emotion removed from it: "It is impossible not to imagine them at their researches, as solemn as a pair of brontosauruses, their heavy old freckled limbs twined about each other, hands probing skillfully for sensitive zones, pigmented areolas, out-of-the-way mucous glands, dormant vascular nexuses. A wave of prickling passes over me such as I have never experienced before" (190).

He sits there, watching the man from St. Louis read his paper, and notices that Kate is shaking like a leaf "because she longs to be an anyone who is anywhere and she cannot." Finally she gets up and staggers from the car. When she has not returned in half an hour, he goes to find her. Still under the effects of his imaginary visit with the Deans, he sits with her in her roomette. He asks if she is all right, and she says she is but proclaims him nuttier than she and accuses him of trying to carry on a marriage with her as "another of his researches." Apparently she thinks he merely wants to see if he can "cure" her. He leaves the roomette and stops in the vestibule for a drink. She joins him. She has just discovered that she is a religious person: "Don't you see? [she asks] What I want is to believe in someone completely and then do what he wants me to do. If God were to tell me: Kate, here is what I want you to do; you get off this train right now and go over there to that corner by the Southern Life and Accident Insurance Company and stand there for the rest of your life and speak kindly to people—you think I wouldn't do it?" (197).

She tells Binx he is the most self-centered person alive, a real compliment to an existentialist, and although she doesn't know that she loves him, she does believe in him. If I marry you, she concludes, you must always tell me what to do. He says he will and she gives him a long passionate kiss. After that kiss, Binx goes into a brown study, and as the train rocks through north Mississippi, they leave spring behind and "the moon hangs westering and yellow over winter fields as blackened and ancient and haunted as battle fields." The change of climate reflects Kate's mood, too, and she moans, "Let's go to your roomette." It's made up for sleeping and they have to lie side-by-side on the narrow bunk. "Feeling tender toward her," Binx tells her he loves her, but she stiffens and says "Oh no . . . none of that bunko. . . . No love please." When he tries to leave, she draws him back and tells him she has consulted her psychiatrist about a little fling, "a Frenchy version" of Mac and Tillie in the stockroom when they are caught by Whipple. Then Kate says, "Now, I'll tell you what you can do Whipple. You get out of here and come back in exactly five minutes." Binx describes their attempt at lovemaking:

> I'll have to tell you the truth, Rory, painful though it is. Nothing would please me more than to say that I had done one of two things. Either that I did what you do: tuck Debbie in your bed and, with a show of virtue so victorious as to be ferocious, grab pillow and blanket and take to the living room sofa, there to lie in the dark, hands clasped behind head, gaze at the ceiling and talk through the open door of your hopes and dreams. Or—do what a hero in a novel would do: he too is a seeker and a pilgrim of sorts and he is just in from Guanajuato or Sambuco where he has found the Real Right Thing or from the East where he apprenticed himself to a wise man and became proficient in

the seventh path to the seventh happiness. Yet he does not disdain this world either and when it happens that a maid comes to his bed with a heart full of longing for him, he puts down his book in a good and cheerful spirit and gives her as merry a time as she could possibly ask for. . . .

No, Rory, I did neither. We did neither. We did very badly and almost did not do at all. Flesh poor flesh failed us. The burden was too great and flesh poor flesh neither hallowed by sacrament nor despised by spirit . . . but until this moment seen through and concealed, rendered null by the cold and fishy eye of the malaise—flesh poor flesh now at this moment summoned all at once to be all and everything, end all and be all, the last and only hope—quails and fails.

. . . .

Good night, sweet Whipple, good night night, good night. (199–200)

It is obvious that Binx is not Don Juan, nor was he meant to be.

This scene is surely the climax of the novel. Almost everything Percy has been hinting at to this point is revealed dramatically here. First of all, it reveals how much Walker Percy's attitude toward community values differs from that of William Faulkner and Allen Tate. Like Flannery O'Connor, Percy once said he did not consider himself a southern novelist, that he used "the Southern scenery, the Southern backdrop, but just as that, as a place where a young man can react." [11] He is writing, he says, fifty years beyond the time of family histories and sagas, but even that explanation does not penetrate the barrier that separates him from the great southern writers of the previous generation, and the durability of his art rests in his ability to confront the basic concerns of his day as they did those of theirs. Tate's Lacy Buchan feels he cannot become personally involved with Jane Posey because family honor and loyalty prohibit his pursuing his interest in a young lady whom his older brother has already decided to court. Bayard Sartoris is so ashamed that he has returned the passionate kiss of his young stepmother that he is bound by honor

11 *Ibid.*, 54.

to reveal his duplicity to his father. When Colonel Sartoris does not seem appalled at his son's confession, Bayard is convinced that his father is no longer following the code that governs civilized behavior. Binx's concerns are aroused by a different system of values. On the surface it would seem that he is confronted with a perfect rotation—"experiencing the new beyond the expectation of experiencing the new"—but he cannot take advantage of it, and the question is why? We know Binx is physically attracted to Kate; he has already commented on her trim ankles and her attractive derriere. She is no blood relation of his, and the fact that she is a stepcousin surely does not concern him at all. The truth is: he had been subjected to the possibility of physical intimacy with the most attractive woman he knows, and he is unable to function. Now this reaction is a matter of real importance to the young man who has managed to avoid the abyss of everydayness in large part by the physical stimulation he receives from associating with a series of attractive secretaries. If he can't respond to the allurement of a sensory experience, he has lost the possibility of the "Little Way . . . the sad little happiness of drinks, kisses" and physical stimulus. He does not feel like the scoundrel that Aunt Emily thinks he should, but it would seem that the means by which he has maintained himself on the aesthetic level and managed to avoid the malaise may be slipping from him. What has actually happened to Binx, however, as he will later realize, is that "poor flesh" failed him, the "Little Way" is no longer satisfactory, because he cannot have a pure, uncluttered physical relationship with Kate. His feeling toward her involves more complicated human emotions. In Ransom's terms, she has become "a person and an aesthetic object." What he feels for her is more than mere animal lust; it includes, as well, that complicated and interconnected mass of human emotions that combine to become human love. To him she has become not anyone but a someone. The establishment of this basic and uniquely human relationship with

Kate—together with the sincere compassion for Lonnie—foreshadow his ultimate abandonment of the aesthetic mode of existence.

In Chicago "the five million personal rays of Chicagoans and the peculiar smell of existence" beat him down, for he knew "no facts about where he was"—no concrete particularities—Who built the station? When? Under what circumstances? He is so completely submerged in everydayness that he feels like No one Nowwhere. He and Kate go out to see Harold Graebner's place in Wilmette, for Harold, who had saved Binx's life in Korea, is one of the few people whom he knows in Chicago. As he walks along the streets and sees the "noble Midwestern girls with their clear eyes and splendid butts," he realizes that he is not aroused at all, that for the first time since he can recall he is free of physical desire. The effect of the experience in the sleeping car goes much deeper than he suspects. The conflicting modern views toward sex, when fornication is no longer regarded as a sin, is an indication of a sick society:

> What a sickness it is [he says]. . . . This latterday Christian sex. To be pagan it would be one thing, an easement taken easily in an old pagan world; to be Christian it would be another thing, fornication forbidden and not even to be thought of in the new life, and I can see that it need not be thought of if there were such a life. But to be neither pagan nor Christian but this: oh this is a sickness. . . . Wherein . . . there are dreamed not one but two American dreams: of Ozzie and Harriet, more than Christian folks, and of Tillie and Mac and belly to back. (207)

That he is not affected by the "noble Midwestern girls" worries him, but he makes a discovery that eases his concern somewhat. In a small bar near their hotel he *discovers* Kate. "There I see her plain, see plain for the first time since I lay wounded in a ditch and watched an Oriental finch scratching around in the leaves—a quiet little body she is, a tough little city Celt; no, more of a Rachael really, a dark little Rachael bound home to Brooklyn on the IRT. I gave her a pat on the leg" (206). She is no longer a part of his problem, a sexless abstraction, a worrisome relative, a mere handsome girl with a "beautiful derriere." All of those abstractions have been replaced by a highly individualized portrait of "a tough little city Celt, a dark little Rachael." He realizes now that in the sleeping car he took the first step toward establishing with her a selfless relationship, one that could move him into the state of intersubjectivity in which their two consciousnesses can be unified.

When they return to the hotel after their visit to Harold's —Binx is hopelessly immured in everydayness—they find a request to return a call to Aunt Emily, who tells them to come home immediately. Kate takes care of all the details of their return trip by bus—the only kind of transportation they can get because of Mardi Gras—and they begin the long trek back to New Orleans to face the ire of Aunt Emily. She is beyond the state of exasperation and simple anger because she has been "worried sick," not knowing where Kate was for the past three days. Emily's argument when she confronts Binx after his return is so sensible and logical, Percy says, "that people in the South think that's the best part of the book, where Aunt Emily tells Binx off . . . and they give me credit for coinciding with Aunt Emily." [12] The truth of the matter, of course, is that Binx, though extremely polite, attentive, and respectful, understands not a word Emily says; at least he can see no relevance her spiel has for him. Her argument is that of *noblesse oblige*, of paternalism—the basic attitude that Percy attributed to his foster father in his introduction to William Alexander Percy's *Lanterns on the Levee*. "Is it a bad thing," Walker Percy asks, "for a man to believe," as W. A. Percy evidently did, "that his position in society entails a certain responsibility toward others . . . for a man to care like a father

12 *Ibid.*, 48.

for his servants, spend himself on the poor, the sick, the miserable?" W. A. Percy believed these things, even as Emily does, and his philosophy of life, like hers, embraced a view of the world "as tragic as it was noble." [13] Readers of *Lanterns on the Levee* can surely see that Walker Percy is putting Will Percy's words in Emily Cutrer's mouth as she gives Binx his dressing down. Throughout history, she says, men who occupied a certain position have behaved in a predictable way: "They display courage, fear, embarrassment, joy, sorrow. . . . Such anyhow has been the funded experience of the race for two or three thousand years, has it not? Your discovery, as best as I can determine, is that there is an alternative which no one has hit upon. It is that one finding oneself in one of life's critical situations need not after all respond in one of the traditional ways. No. One may simply default. Pass. Do as one pleases, shrug, turn on one's heel and leave. Exit" (220). Although Aunt Emily's tone is sarcastic, she is closer to stating Binx's view of the truth than she suspects. Even as she is accusing him of the most despicable behavior she can imagine, he is very much aware of Who and Where he is—the specific house noises, the muted voices of the servants going about their everyday assignments, the strained behavior of his Uncle Jules, saying his good morning "briefly and sorrowfully as if the furtherest limit of his disapproval lay in the brevity of his greeting" (220). Binx's manners, however, are impeccable. He apologizes for his aunt's not being informed of Kate's going to Chicago with him. She accuses him of not being able to care for anyone and asks, obviously fearful of the answer she might receive, a question concerning what would be to her an unimaginable horror. "Were you intimate with Kate?" Binx responds as truthfully as he can: "Not very" for "intimate is not quite the word." His aunt almost explodes: "Intimate is not quite the word? I wonder what is the word. You see . . .

13 Introduction, William Alexander Percy, *Lanterns on the Levee* (Baton Rouge: Louisiana State University Press, 1973), 4.

there is another of my hidden assumptions. All of these years
I have been assuming that between us words mean roughly
the same thing, that among certain people, gentlefolk I don't
mind calling them, there exists a set of meanings held in common, that a certain manner and certain grace come as naturally as breathing" (222).

Binx can think of nothing to say and remains silent. "Don't
you live by these things," she asks, and he says, "No'm." With
a turn of her back, she dismisses him and he leaves the house.
Kate sees him leave and tells him to wait for her at his house.
As he makes his way back to Gentilly, he remembers it is his
thirtieth birthday and declares he has learned only one thing
in his thirty years and that is to recognize merde when he sees
it. In this time of scientific humanism everyone becomes an
anyone, men are dead, "the malaise has settled down like a
fall-out and what people fear is not that the bomb will fall
but that the bomb will not fall" (228).

Nothing remains, he thinks, but desire. After his talk with
his aunt, his search is forgotten and abandoned. All he wants,
he believes, is a girl, any girl. So he calls Sharon and when he
finds her out with her fiancé (her approaching marriage star-
tles him), he begins to talk to her roommate, Joyce, growing
highly excited over the prospects of a new alliance. Just as she
is inviting him over Saturday evening in her most seductive
voice, he looks across the street and sees Kate driving up. With
dramatic clarity he instantly realizes he can no longer settle
for the "Little Way." He knows it's not *any* girl he wants but
one girl, Kate. He concludes his telephone conversation, therefore, with a request: "May I," he asks, "bring along my own
fiancée? I want you and Sharon to meet her" (231).

He tells Kate he must go to see his aunt, for he has promised to tell her what he intends to do. Kate says she has already
told her stepmother that they plan to marry and asks him what
does he plan to do. He responds: "There is only one thing I
can do: listen to people, see how they stick themselves into

the world, hand them along a ways in their dark journey and be handed along, and for good and selfish reasons" (233). This statement is as close to Christian existentialism as Percy ever gets. Certainly it agrees with his assertion that the vocation of a novelist is "writing about man in transit, man as pilgrim." [14]

The question is, finally, what has Percy told us about the nature of man, for he says that he became a novelist only after he was convinced that science cannot tell man "What he is and what he must do." We know Binx is in a predicament, and with the most intense probing of the recesses of his inner being, Percy reveals to us exactly how his character feels about everything he experiences. Still we are not quite certain how far Percy has handed Binx along on his dark journey. There is some evidence—and Robert Coles believes this is the extent of Binx's journey—to suggest that he has moved from Kierkegaard's aesthetic mode to his ethical mode: He is aware of Kate as an individual (not just as someone with a problem), and he wants her, despite his traumatic experience on the train; he knows by marrying her he can help her through her illness—he can be the solid foundation on which she can build her life. Percy says that someone must tell her what to do, that her and Binx's relationship is almost one of "hypnotic suggestion." [15] Binx may be going to medical school not merely to please his aunt but because he knows that only by acquiring certain technical knowledge can he help the Lonnies of the world. (After all, Lonnie's fatal illness is never specifically diagnosed.) This kind of reasoning would seem to indicate that Binx has merely moved from the basement to the first floor of Kierkegaard's house, from the aesthetic mode to the ethical mode, that he has moved from selfishness toward selflessness and intersubjectivity. Then through a leap of faith,

14 Carr (ed.), *Kite-Flying*, 46.   15 *Ibid.*, 47.

which might occur in the future, he could land in the center of the religious realm.

Percy insists, however, that he plots Binx's journey through life at a different pace, and his argument of Binx's position at the end of the novel, even allowing for the intentional fallacy, is convincing. The ending of the novel, Percy tells John Carr, is a salute to Dostoevsky's *The Brothers Karamazov*. As Alyosha does in that novel when Koyla dies, Binx tells his half-brothers and -sisters that Lonnie is going to die but that they will see him again on judgment day, well and no longer crippled. "In the end," Percy says, "Binx jumps from the aesthetic clear across the ethical to the religious. He has no ethical sphere at all. That's what Aunt Emily can't understand about him. He just doesn't believe in being the honorable man, doing the right thing for its own sake." Binx does say he can do what he has to do either from a service station, which he considers buying, or from the profession of medicine, which his aunt wants him to pursue. It would seem that Binx's position at the end of the novel is the direct result of his changing attitude toward Kate and his respect for Lonnie's unquestioned faith. Regardless of where Binx is on the scale of being at the end of the novel, he has moved from where he was at its beginning. Percy has demonstrated conclusively that "man is neither an organism controlled by his environment, nor a creature controlled by the forces of history as the Marxists would say, nor is he a detached, wholly objective, angelic being who views the world in a godlike way and makes pronouncements only to himself or to an elite group of people." [16] Although he could not accept the paternalism of W. A. Percy and Aunt Emily, as Tate and Faulkner to a large extent could, neither did he find Sartre's atheism or political activism any more compatible than he did nihilism; Percy's search for man's

16 *Ibid.*, 49, 46.

place in an absurd world led him finally to accept the integrity and the transcendent nature of the individual human spirit. The intent of his fiction is not that of Flannery O'Connor's, nor is its tone, but its effect is not as different as some readers seem to believe.

VIII Terminal: John Barth's The End of the Road

In the opening sentence of *The End of the Road*, John Barth warns us that the Jacob Horner, who writes from his hospital bed, may be quite different from the character by the same name who participates in the narrative that he develops.[1] For there are, as the narrator tells us repeatedly, many Jake Horners, and sometimes there is no Jake Horner at all. At the end of his encounter with the Morgans and the Doctor, it seems certain, as Jac Tharpe points out, that all that remains of Jake is an "anguished hulk of protoplasm that left the bust of Laocoön behind after carefully moving it with him, because he had become Laocoön."[2] There seems to be a strong suggestion that he has come as close as any character in contemporary literature to losing his self-identity, his realization of who he is and where he is from, for Horner's self may cease to exist as soon as he completes his narrative. The teller, even the label *Jacob Horner*, may exist only in the tale.

Jacob the narrator can see in Jacob the character several distinct persons, and sometimes no person at all, depending upon his

1 John Barth, *The End of the Road* (New York: Grosset and Dunlap, 1971), 1. All references are to this edition, and page numbers will be given in the text.
2 Jac Tharpe, *John Barth: The Comic Sublimity* (Carbondale: Southern Illinois University Press, 1977), 24. In *Letters* (New York: Putnam's, 1979), Barth assures us that Horner is alive but not well, residing on the Farm in Eana at the opposite side of the Peace Bridge from Buffalo.

mood or the weather or the attitude he can read into the fixed expression on the statue of Laocoön. Rennie Morgan accuses Jake of being less than an identifiable human being because he has no firmly held intellectual and ethical positions. Immediately after Jake and her husband Joe first meet, she tells Jake she is uncomfortable because she is not really sure that Joe is stronger than he, and she lives so much on Joe's strength that she feels threatened. Then she is relieved because she can easily see that when Joe has destroyed one of Jake's positions:

> [He] hadn't really touched *you*—there wasn't that much of you in any of your positions.
> . . . .
> You know what I've come to think, Jake? I think you don't exist at all. There's too many of you. It's more than just masks that you put on and take off—we all have masks. But you're different all the way through, every time. You cancel yourself out. You're more like someone in a dream. You're not strong and you're not weak. You're nothing.
> . . . .
> I've decided I don't have to think about you or deal with you anymore, because you don't exist. (62–63)

One of Jake's nightmares is a dream in which he is told there will be no weather today. Weather is important to him because *he* is the mood he adopts at a particular moment and that mood is Jake Horner. Although a day without weather is unthinkable, there are many days in which he has no mood at all. On these days, he says, it is as Rennie has guessed, as if there is no Jake Horner at all, that "except in a meaningless metabolistic sense" Jacob Horner ceases to exist (33). Jake is aware that "there is little of him" in the positions he takes in his arguments with Joe: "Some days I was a stock left-wing Democrat, other days I professed horror at the concept of reform in anything; some days I was ascetic, some days Rabelaisian; some days super-rational, some days anti-rational" (61). Except on his "weatherless" days he vehemently defends whatever position that he has adopted because "it was as good a way as any to kill the afternoon." Jacob the narrator, then, is aware of the indefinite changeable character of Jacob the actor. After Joe has told Rennie that he wants her to know Jake because he wants her to become acquainted with a first-rate mind besides his, Rennie says to Jake: "What scares me sometimes is that in a number of ways you are *not* totally different from Joe. . . . I've even heard the same sentences from each of you at different times." With that remark, Jake says, "my mood changed as if by magic. I was now a strong, quiet, half-sinister Jacob Horner, nothing like the wise-cracking fop who'd heard the earlier part of Rennie's history" (59).

Jacob Horner's inability to identify himself makes him a postmodern, a contemporary man. He has other traits that unerringly place him among his contemporaries. John Barth once told an interviewer that in addition to the obvious connections between *Horner* and *cuckold*, "someone who puts horns on," Jake is intended to suggest the nursery rhyme character "who sits in his corner and rationalizes."[3] Barth, or his narrator Jacob Horner, has afflicted his character with a uniquely contemporary malaise, "Cosmopsis": he views the whole but ignores the details. He has, in Allen Tate's words, only the "long view of history"; therefore he can never see a "whole horse," only an abstract configuration of the concrete object. In Percy's terms he is unaware of the concrete particularities of the world around him and, therefore, he is always anyone living anywhere. His view of things is so broad that he can conceive of nothing he can do that would change anything in the world in which he exists. He doesn't commit suicide because he can think of no rational reason to do so. Nothing is worth doing because all human action is valueless. He is engulfed in despair because, in Kierkegaard's words, he is "unaware of being in despair." Locked in the aesthetic mode with no hope of ascending beyond it, his search—if he were to undertake one—would have to be a vertical search because of his inclination to rationalize and his obliviousness to the sensuous world around him. He has neither the conviction, nor the courage, nor the motivation to make a choice.

2

On March 16, 1951, Jacob Horner withdraws from Johns Hopkins University, in which he had enrolled the previous September, and goes to the Pennsylvania Station in Baltimore with a little more than thirty dollars in his pocket. After inquiring from the ticket agent where he could go on that amount of money and receiving several possible destinations, he sits on a bench trying to choose among them. Completely immobile, unable even to focus his eyes, he is found early on the morning of March 17, after maintaining the same position for more than twelve hours—his eyes "sightless, gazing on eternity, fixed on ultimacy"—by a "small, dapper black man of fifty," who breaks his trance and sends him for coffee. He soon comes to know this man as the Doctor, accompanies him to his Rehabilitation Farm, and begins therapy for his immobility. First there is Informational therapy, learning facts from the *World Almanac*. "Choosing is existence," the Doctor says; "to the extent you don't choose, you don't exist" (77). All of his theories, the Doctor says, are aimed at making one conscious that he exists. It doesn't matter that your actions are neither constructive nor consistent so long as you act. It doesn't matter that your character isn't admirable, so long as you have one.

That the Doctor is little concerned with values is clear, and it becomes even more apparent in the instructions he gives Jake as he leaves the farm: Jake should not believe in God because religion would only make him despondent, but it might help if he would read Sartre and become an existentialist (the reason for his suggestion becomes evident in a later discussion). He should continue to read the *World Almanac*; he should take a job, preferably in a factory but not one simple enough to allow him to think coherently while he works. He should go out, play cards with people, read no creative literature except plays, watch no television, and exercise frequently, taking long walks but always knowing his destination before leaving his house. Above all, Jake must act impulsively; he should never get stuck between two alternatives. If the alternatives are side by side, he should take the one to the left (Sinistrality); if they are consecutive in time, he should choose the earlier (Antecedence). If neither of these applies, he should choose the alternative that begins with the earlier letter in the alphabet (Alphabetical Priority). Obviously, the Doctor is demonstrating his belief that action, regardless of its value or consequence, is essence.

Jake follows the Doctor's orders as closely as he can. He gets a job on an assembly line in a Chevrolet factory, operating an air wrench that bolts leaf springs onto the chassis of the car; he reads Sartre (but not too enthusiastically), takes walks, plays poker with some acquaintances from the plant, uses Sinistrality, Antecedence, and Alphabetical Priority as the means of choosing between alternatives, and for two years lives an uneventful life, one in which he is completely submerged in everydayness. At the end of that time, in June, 1953, he goes back to see the Doctor, who tells him he should take a real job, a vocation with a definite future. After a brief discussion of Jake's qualifications, it is decided that he should take a position teaching prescriptive—not descriptive—grammar at Wicomico State Teachers College. Under no circumstances is he to teach literature. Again he is not to be caught between alternatives, because in prescriptive grammar there will always be a rule to determine for him what is right and what is wrong.

Jake receives an appointment teaching prescriptive grammar and composition (the Doctor is displeased when he learns about the composition, but Jake insists he had to take it in or-

der to get the grammar). Since it is June and classes do not begin until September, Jake settles into his rented room to wait
out the summer. Soon, however, he becomes friends with Joe
Morgan, a young history instructor, and his wife Rennie. In
Joe, Jake sees a man who has taken an entirely different view
of how one should act in a world in which there is no purpose, no cohesive center to hold it together. Joe has devised a
system to give aim and direction to his life when for most men
there seems to be no constructive way in which they can expend their energy. Jake has long since decided that in a world
devoid of absolute values, no action is worth the effort, and
only by adhering to the Doctor's arbitrary system is he able to
act at all. His Cosmopsis, his "Long View of History," allows
him to see the world only as a vast desert of nothingness.

Since there are no absolutes, Joe argues, one must adopt
certain relative values and treat them as if they were absolute.
Joe's orientation is neither conventional nor Christian, and
the principal relative value he has converted to an absolute is
his marriage to Rennie: "The most important thing in the
world to me—one of my absolutes, I suppose—[he tells
Jake] is the relationship between Rennie and me" (107). Since
there is no system of values outside of man by which he can
judge the worthiness of his own actions, he must be absolutely
certain that all of his actions are consciously motivated (note
that in the Doctor's system, action is mechanically set in motion and controlled), rationally explainable (this is the one that
will later destroy his marriage), consistent, and "lived out"
to the letter. He explains to Jake how this last characteristic
works out in actual practice:

> There's no sense in apologizing, because nothing is ultimately defensi-
> ble. But a man can act coherently; he can act in ways that he can ex-
> plain, if he wants to. This is important to me. Do you know, for the
> first month of our marriage Rennie used to apologize all over herself
> to friends who dropped in, because we didn't have much furniture in
> the house. She knew very well that we didn't want any more furniture

even if we could have afforded it, but she always apologized to other
people for not having their point of view. One day she did it more
elaborately than usual, and as soon as the company left I popped her
one on the jaw. Laid her out cold. When she came to, I explained to
her very carefully why I'd hit her. She cried, and apologized to me for
having apologized to other people. I popped her again. (43–44)

Jake notes that there was no "boastfulness in Joe's voice . . .
neither was there any regret."

The final criterion Joe sets for his relative values is that
they be taken seriously. "You shouldn't consider a value less
real because it isn't absolute," Joe tells Jake, "since less than
absolutes are all we've got" (39). Again, he comes to his marriage, saying it is no less real just because it isn't absolute. It's
important to him because he has decided for himself the conditions under which marriage is important to him:

I'm not a man who needs to be married under any circumstances—in
fact, under a lot of circumstances I couldn't tolerate being married—
and one of my conditions for preserving any relationship at all, but
particularly a marriage relationship, would be that the parties involved
be able to take each other seriously. If I straighten Rennie out now
and then, or tell her some statement of hers is stupid as hell, or even
slug her one, it's because I respect her and to me that means not making
a lot of kinds of allowances for her. Making allowances might be Christian, but to me it would always mean not taking seriously the person
you make allowances for. (42)

The system that Joe devises to give some kind of order to
an absurd universe and provide a means by which he can attach a scale of values to human behavior is, of course, a rather
naïve variety of ethical positivism, a system that attaches no
value to anything that cannot be perceived by one or more of
the five senses. He arbitrarily imposes on such phenomena a
basic pragmatic scheme that gives the illusion of being both
practical and ideal. It's the kind of thinking, Ransom says, that
some poets employ, those who don't actually believe that the
image is an authentic means of cognition. Since they feel in
some vague way that poetry must have images, however, they

use them to illustrate ideas. Joe believes that life must contain standards, what he calls "givens," and since there are no longer any absolutes, he selects *some* relative values and lets them *represent* absolutes. The narrator of the novel, *that* Jacob Horner, quickly sees the fallacy in Joe's thinking. He has adopted a role—that of the rationalist in an irrational world —and tries to make all human experience—conscious and unconscious, plausible and implausible, deliberate and automatic—fit his preconceived pattern of the way human beings should act. Although his antics before the mirror on the night Rennie and Jake spy on him demonstrate that role-playing is an important part of his life, as it is of everyone else's, this fact is inconceivable to him because of the positivistic structure he has imposed on human behavior. If one looks at his views from another angle, he can easily see how Joe reduces concrete, individualistic human behavior to abstract qualities, another way of relying upon what Percy has called the method of science: rationalism can explain everything about a man except "what he is in himself." There are only four things that Joe is not impressed with, he says: "unity, harmony, eternality and universality." The only index to man's desires is "in his acts: What a man did is what he wanted to do." Jake's only response to this impressive summary of an attitude toward life is to say that he would have recoiled from so systematic an analysis of things even if God had informed him that "such seemed to be the case."

Soon after this conversation occurs—and maybe it was a series of conversations, since Jake says he cannot be certain—Joe arranges to have Rennie teach Jake to ride so that she will have the opportunity to see his "first-class mind" in action. During these rides, and while they are resting the horses, Jake listens to Rennie talk about her attitude toward her marriage. She was nothing, she says, "lived in a complete fog," until she met Joe. All the way through school and college she slept, had no thoughts, no fun. In one marathon session after she meets

Joe in New York, he explains to her what he expects from a "more or less permanent" relationship with a woman, that they will stay together only "as long as each of us respects everything about the other." Rennie says she "completely erased" herself so that she could start all over. She thinks of Joe, Jake can see, as one would think of God, and when Jake asks about her self-identity, about the disappearance of her individuality, she says that she has lost nothing, that she had rather be a "lousy Joe Morgan than a first-rate Rennie Mac-Mahon."

Rennie is obviously no match for either Joe or Jake, and as the novel develops, although she insists that her adoration of Joe is unshaken by Jake's cynical sophistry, she admits that she becomes more uncertain of her feelings toward Jake. "I may love you," she admits at one point, "but I also hate your guts." The novel can be read, as Jac Tharpe points out, almost like a medieval morality play, with God and Satan vying for the soul of a single individual:

> Joe is God for the innocent Rennie until she, like Ambrose in *Lost in the Funhouse*, peers through the crack in the enclosure. But eating the fruit of the tree of knowledge is what shattered Eve's illusions, and the helpmeet made from the man's rib became the source of his unhappiness. Yet, so long as Joe does appear sufficiently invincible even to support a caricature of himself, he sustains an order sufficient for being that is nothingness, until nothingness reveals that being is nothingness.[4]

Perhaps Tharpe has slightly overstated his case; it is obvious, nevertheless, that Rennie is intellectual pap for Joe and Jake. Although the debate is articulated in religious terms (Jake alludes to himself as the devil's advocate), much earlier in the conflict Rennie sees that the differences between Joe and Jake are more apparent than real. She has "erased" herself and adopted one position, Joe's, but in the ensuing struggle she takes on more and more of Jake's characteristics and

4 Tharpe, *The Comic Sublimity*, 32.

becomes less and less like Joe, until finally, like Jake, she is confronted not with a single choice but with many choices, all of which appear equally valid. On one occasion, Jake says, "it was never much of a chore for me, at various times, to maintain with perfectly equal unenthusiasm contradictory, or at least polarized, opinions on a given subject" (114). At her lowest moment Rennie admits: "That's one of the things that destroys me . . . the idea that I might have been in love with you . . . occurred to me along with all the rest—along with the idea I despise you" (133). Like Jake, too, she is immobilized. Holding so many different opinions, all of which, on the surface at least, seem equally acceptable, she is incapable of making the decisive choice that will result in a definite action. As the Doctor says later, he, Joe, Jake, and perhaps others "bear equal responsibility for Rennie's death." They all violate the sacredness of her person. They all represent different kinds of nonbelief, and Rennie's sense of selfhood, never very strong, cannot withstand their combined assault.

A few days before school begins, and the day before his night with Rennie, Jake makes his periodic visit to the Farm. The Doctor immediately senses a change in Jake's attitude and asks him, "Who is the confident fellow you've befriended?" (82). Jake tells him it's none of his business, and the Doctor, after commenting on his assertive new behavior, tells him he's ready for Mythotherapy, which Jake has been unconsciously practicing all the time. As the Doctor describes Mythotherapy, one can see why earlier he had encouraged Jake to read Sartre:

> Mythotherapy is based on two assumptions: that human existence precedes human essence . . . and that a man is free not only to choose his own essence but to change it at will.
>
> . . . .
>
> In life there are no essentially major or minor characters. . . . Everyone is necessarily the hero of his own life story. *Hamlet* could be told from Polonius's point of view and called *The Tragedy of Polonius, Lord Chamberlain of Denmark*. . . . Or suppose you are an usher in a wedding. From the groom's point of view he's the major character; the

others play supporting parts, even the bride. From your viewpoint, though, the wedding is a minor episode in the very interesting history of *your* life, and the bride and groom both are minor figures. What you've done is to choose *to play the part* of a minor character: it can be pleasant for you *to pretend to be* less important than you know you are, as Odysseus does when he disguises as a swineherd.

. . . .

If any man displays almost the same character day in and day out, all day long, it's either because he has no imagination, like an actor who plays only one role, or because he has an imagination so comprehensive that he sees each particular situation of his life as an episode in some grand over-all plot. (82–83)

Although it would appear useless to try to determine in which of the two last-named categories the Doctor would place Joe, we know that Joe, after considerable thought has concluded that he will play one role, that of the Ethical Pragmatist or the Ethical Positivist. Jake, on the other hand, has played many different roles—that of the Dedicated Teacher before the Wicomico State Teachers College employment committee, that of the Fresh but Unintelligent Young Man in his first encounter with Peggy Rankin, and that of devil's advocate, among others, in his conversations with Joe. During his first days of classes he found the air of his classroom "electric with sex like ozone after a summer storm"; consequently by four he "had so abandoned" himself to erotic desire that he is virtually in pain. After his last class, therefore, he seeks out Peggy Rankin, a forty-year-old English teacher with whom he has had a most unsatisfactory sexual encounter a few weeks before. (It is most significant that Rennie does not occur to him as a sexual partner, although they have had their night less than a week before.) He rushes to the high school, tells Peggy he must see her at once (She protests, "Jake, for God's sake, are you just picking me up again?") and proceeds to put the Doctor's theory to work, this time playing the role of Joe Morgan. Peggy says she thinks Jake is a monster and asks how he can even look at her after the way he treated her the last time. Jake's response is a paraphrase of Joe's words, and a ludicrous imitation of his technique, in his courtship of Rennie. "I'm afraid I overestimated you, Peggy," Jake says, "I thought after I met you that you might actually be the superior woman you give the first impression of being. But you know, you're turning out to be one hundred per cent ordinary" (90). Peggy's reaction to this statement, that Jake has no "common respect for a woman's dignity," really triggers the Joe Morgan-like response:

> That's it, right there . . . a common respect, a common courtesy, a common this, a common that. Add it all up and what it gives you is a common relationship, and that's a thing I've no use for. You don't seem to be my kind of girl, Peggy, and I could have sworn you were. My kind of girl doesn't want common respect; she wants uncommon respect, and that means a relationship where nobody makes the common allowances for anybody else.
>
> . . . .
>
> Chivalry is a fiction invented by men who don't want to be bothered with taking women seriously. The minute a man and a woman assent to it they stop thinking of each other as individual human beings: they assent to it precisely so they won't have to think about their partners. Which is completely useful, of course, if sex is the only thing that's on your mind. I may as well tell you, Peggy, now that it's too late, that you're the only woman I ever dared try to respect before, and take completely seriously, on my own terms, just as I'd take myself. (97)

When Peggy bursts into nervous laughter, Jake, in true Joe Morgan fashion, turns from the steering wheel and "very carefully" socks her on the cheek. "Try to understand, Peggy, that I'm not that interested in laying women. I can do without. [He's coming close to Joe's words now.] But I will not have my deepest values thrown in my face." Peggy's reaction is much like Rennie's, "I'll die if you say it's too late." He tantalizes her a little more by saying, "I really was just bringing you home. . . . When may I see you again?" She is amazed by this remark, as Jake knew she would be, and almost literally drags him into her apartment, saying "Oh, Jake, *now*!" The parody of Joe's courtship of Rennie is finished.

3

Jake's riding lessons continue almost to the opening of school. Soon after they begin, the rides start to follow a specific pattern. They ride for about an hour, then dismount in a little cove, and rest for ten or fifteen minutes. Almost inevitably Rennie begins to talk about her marriage: how she and Joe once spent two days and two nights talking about what they expected from marriage. Joe, who did most of the talking, insisted that "anything we did together we had to do on the same level." What their lengthy dialogue amounted to, finally, was a relationship as devoid of emotional substance as Joe's rational obsession could make it. After one emotional session with Jake in the cove, in which Rennie says she sometimes thinks Joe arranged the meetings between Jake and her because he wanted "the Devil to test me, too," she completely breaks down and sobs uncontrollably, her teeth actually chattering. Jake strokes her hair and tries to console her. When he thinks she has regained her composure sufficiently, they start home, hoping to arrive about the time Joe returns from a Boy Scout meeting.

They stop in Rennie's yard, for Jake realizes that she is still crying, and he suggests that they wait outside a minute before going into the living room where Joe is presumably working on his dissertation. As they wait, Jake invites Rennie to eavesdrop with him, saying it's great to see the "animals in their natural habitat." She says, "You disgust me, Jake. . . . He's just reading. You don't know Joe at all, do you?" But she reluctantly peeps in with Jake and what she sees changes her opinion of Joe, destroys her marriage, and ultimately leads to her death:

Joe Morgan, back from his Boy Scout meeting, had evidently intended to do some reading, for there were books lying open on the writing table and on the floor beside the bookcase. But Joe wasn't reading. He was standing in the exact center of the bare room, fully dressed, smartly executing military commands. About *face*! Right *dress*! Ten-*shun*! Parade *rest*! He saluted briskly, his cheeks blown out and his tongue extended, and then proceeded to cavort about the room—spinning, pirouetting, bowing, leaping, kicking. I watched entranced by his performance, for I cannot say that in my strangest moments (and a bachelor has strange ones) I have surpassed him. Rennie trembled from head to foot.

Ah! passing a little mirror on the wall, Joe caught his own eye. What? What? Ahoy there! He stepped close, curtsied to himself and thrust his face to within two inches of the glass. Mr. Morgan, is it? Howdy do, Mr. Morgan. Blah bloo blah. Oo-o-o-o bubble thlwurp. He mugged antic faces at himself, sklurching up his eye corners, zblooging his mouth about, glubbing his cheeks, Mither Morgle. Nyoing nyang nyumpie. Vglibble vglobble vglup. Vgliggy*bloo*! Thlucky thlucky, thir.

He jabbed his spectacles back on his nose. Had he heard some sound? No. He went to the writing table and apparently resumed his reading, his back turned to us. The show, then, was over. Ah, but one moment—yes. He turned slightly, and we could see: his tongue gripped purposefully between his lips at the side of his mouth. Joe Morgan was masturbating and picking his nose at the same time. I believe he also hummed a sprightly tune in rhythm with his work. (65–66) [5]

As Rennie observes these antics from the man whose every action, she has believed, is the logical result of incisive rational thought, she can only press her forehead against the window sill, while Jake speaks softly "in her ear the worldless grammarless language she'd taught me to calm horses with" (66). There is no doubt but that Joe's godhood is destroyed.

5 Some commentators have wondered why this obviously crucial scene is never mentioned again. It seems to me that when Rennie observes Joe's antics when he thinks he is alone, her suspicions are confirmed: there are no essential differences between Jake and Joe. This conclusion could account for her subsequent infidelity. Her loss of faith in Joe as a distinct individualized human being destroys her belief in the sanctity of the agreement she made with him. All of Rennie's subsequent actions are motivated by the effect on her of what she sees through the window.

Three days after they have observed Joe's antics, he goes to Washington to do some research for his dissertation at the Library of Congress. Before leaving he asks Jake to keep his eye on Rennie and the boys while he is gone. On the first afternoon of Joe's absence, Jake goes over to the Morgan apartment, plays with the boys, and Rennie asks him to stay for dinner. There was nothing at all compromising, he later decides, about his going out to see Rennie and the boys; least of all were his actions sexually motivated, for, he says, he "was never highly sexed." On that evening he "was neither bored nor fatigued nor sad nor excited nor fresh nor happy: merely a placid animal" (92). There was no hint of suggestivity in Rennie's invitation for dinner, nor was there any particular reason why he should not have eaten in a restaurant. The meal itself was most uneventful and nothing about the evening was planned or prearranged:

> We scarcely spoke to each other. Rennie said once, "I feel lost without Joe," but I could think of no appropriate reply, and for that matter I was not certain how extensive was the intended meaning of her observation. After dinner I volunteered to oversee the boys' bath, spun them a bedtime story and bade them good night. I could have left then, but my staying to drink ale with Rennie during the evening certainly had no clear significance.
>
> . . . .
>
> There was no overt act, no word or deed that unambiguously indicated desire on the part of either of us. I shall certainly admit that I found Rennie attractive that day [but] . . . my sexual desire that I felt was more or less abstract. . . .
>
> Then at nine-thirty or thereabouts Rennie said, "I'm going to take a shower and go to bed, Jake," and I said, "All right." To reach the bathroom, she had to go through a little hallway off the living room; to get my jacket, I had to go to an open closet in this same hallway. And so it is not quite necessary to raise an eyebrow at the fact that we got up from our chairs and went to the hallway together. There, if she turned to face me for a slight moment at the door to the bathroom, who's to say confidently that good nights were not on the tips of tongues? It happened that we embraced each other instead before we went our separate ways—but I think a slow-motion camera would not

have shown who moved first—and it happened further (but I would
not say *consequently*) that our separate ways led to the same bed.
(93–94)

The whole business, he insists, meant nothing to him, and in
his description he goes to great length to explain that it was
something that just happened, that there was no premedita-
tion, no conscious planning on the part either of him or of
Rennie. His mood was not one of weatherlessness, he says, it
was first "one of general and later specific desire, combined
with a definite but not inordinate masculine curiosity" (94–
95). Although his participation was not a gratuitous act, nor
was it unmotivated, Jake says he "would call it both specifically (if not generally) unpremeditated and entirely unreflec-
tive. The fellow who committed it was not thinking ahead of
his desire" (95). Our narrator, we recall, is only in a sense
Jacob Horner. He cannot be absolutely certain of the motivations of the character by the same name in the story he is
telling.

After he leaves the Morgan house, life goes on as usual. He
reads plays for five days before school begins, and the erotic
desires aroused by his students on the first day of classes are
satisfied by Peggy Rankin. As he relaxes one evening, Rennie
calls and says it's urgent that he come over immediately while
Joe's at the Scout meeting. Only then does he think of what
he has done: He thinks Rennie's call is an offer to polish "the
crown of thorns we'd already placed on Joe's brow." For the
first time he has an emotional reaction; he feels sick. "What
in heaven's name was I doing?" he asks. "What, for God's
sake had I done? I was appalled. Does Jacob Horner betray
the only man he can think of as a friend, and then double the
felony by concealing the betrayal?" He gets his first intima-
tion of one of the basic weaknesses of the Doctor's theory of
Mythotherapy: it is an overintellectualization of life; it con-
ceives of man's journey as purely an abstract voyage, the abyss
as imaginary and the dragon by the wayside as mere card-

board. Mythotherapy makes no allowance for human emotions; therefore it prohibits the development of close personal relationships.

Jake's apparent burden of guilt crushes him, and he wants to turn back, but he goes on to a darker tragedy than he can imagine. Rennie is completely overcome with grief, and he cannot imagine her wanting to repeat the unspeakable act of a few nights before. She says she would kill herself, but that would just be cheating Joe more. Jake leaves her and finds reading or sleeping impossible; he cannot adopt a role or slip "into someone else's world." Although as always we cannot be certain of the genuineness of Jacob Horner's emotional responses—because even the narrator, the Jacob Horner who tells the story, is unsure—Jake appears for the moment to be concerned about the human beings he has wronged so terribly. The fact that he has convinced himself that the act was not premeditated does not appear to make him feel any less responsible for the suffering he has caused. Before reaching the conclusion that Jake seems to be suggesting, however, we must not forget his admitted inability to *know* his precise feelings, except as the Doctor has taught him; he believes that action is quality, an essence, important in itself, but that the results of that action have no significance. He is not Cass Mastern who would say that he has touched the web of life, and it doesn't matter whether he intended to touch it or not, that the vibrations that ripple even to the remotest perimeter are the result of an action of his. Jake feels, however, that he wants to call Joe or to drive out there and tell him what he has done, but then realizes that he cannot feel remorse, except fleetingly because he has no unchanged self.

Jake's greatest trial lies ahead. He will soon have to assume his most important role. He learns that philosophy is no game with Joe Morgan. Joe lives by what he believes, and he believes man is always capable of performing the coherent act, that a man does what he wants to do. All of man's decisions are made in the face of conflicting desires, and he always does the thing supported by the stronger desire. When Joe asks Jake, therefore, why he *wanted* to sleep with Rennie, Jake's answer is most unsatisfactory. When Jake says, "I didn't *want* to do it," Joe is disgusted. "Maybe you don't *approve* of what you did, but you obviously wanted to," he replies; "what a man ends up doing is what he has to take responsibility for wanting to do. Why did you *think* you were doing it?" Jake tries to say he was not thinking—and obviously he wasn't—that if he had any motives, they must have been unconscious ones, but Joe thinks Jake is trying to be devious and obtuse.

Somewhat to his surprise, Jake momentarily feels a deep sense of guilt, although he is so far from having a definite continuous point of view that he cannot really say he is sorry to have fornicated with the wife of his best friend and then tried to conceal his duplicity. Now that the affair is out in the open —and the three-day rain has stopped—his mood changes, and the prospect of dealing concretely with Joe about the matter alters his feeling of guilt to one of puzzlement. He wonders now what he can do to pacify Joe. He knows he has neither the desire nor the ability to defend what he has done, so he wants to put the whole affair behind him. "The Jacob Horner that I felt a desperate desire to defend," he says, "was not the one who had tumbled stupidly on Joe Morgan's bed with Joe Morgan's wife or the one who had burned in shame and skulking fear for days afterwards, but the one who was now the object of Joe's disgust—the Horner of the present moment and all the Horners to come" (106). He knows, however, that the affair will not be over until Joe is satisfied.

When Joe comes to see Jake, it is evident that he has only one interest. He wants to understand *why* Rennie did what she did. Every act of man has its motivating cause and the only hint he has of what might have been Rennie's motivation for her infidelity is curiosity. She had never slept with any man except Joe, but desire for a different partner is not sufficient cause, he feels, for her violating her strong feelings about marital fidelity. "According to my version of Rennie," he says, "what happened couldn't have happened." His code of ethical pragmatism, of making absolute values out of relative ones when no absolutes exist, has been shattered, and he must know why. The very foundation upon which his whole code of values is based has been destroyed. The center that held his life together has been dissolved, and he is scurrying about as aimlessly as Tate's blind crab. He asks Jake to be honest with him so that he can see if his behavior has influenced her actions. He wants concrete particularities, and Jake can only give abstractions: "I'm sorry, Joe. . . . I take full responsibility for everything that happened" (109). "Do you take full responsibility for the fact," Joe asks, "that she was on top the first time? Was it you that bit yourself on your left shoulder?" Jake can only protest: "Listen, Joe, . . . you've got to allow for the fact that people—maybe yourself excluded—aren't going to have conscious motives for everything they do. There'll always be a few things in their autobiography that they can't account for. Now when that happens the person could still make up conscious reasons—maybe in your case they'd spring to mind the first time you thought about an act after you did it—but they'd always be rationalizations after the fact" (110–11).

As reasonable as Jake's argument seems to be, Joe can accept no part of it. The very cornerstone of his philosophic system, that upon which everything else is constructed, is the premise that there is a motive for every human action; man always does what he wants to do. He is no nearer to finding an answer to his question, and he gets no closer, though he pushes Jake relentlessly: Why did Rennie *want* to be unfaithful? As their discussions proceed, the weaknesses in Joe's ethical position become transparently clear. Jake tells him: "When somebody close to you injures you unaccountably, and you say, 'Why in the world did you do that?' and they say, 'I don't know,' it seems to me that that answer can be worthy of respect. And if it's somebody you love or trust who says it, and they say it contritely, I think it could be acceptable." But Joe can only respond, "Once they're in a position to *have* to say it, how do you tell whether the love and trust that make it acceptable were justified?" (111–12). What is lacking in Joe's system, obviously, is that he does not believe in "knowledge carried to the heart"; there is no place in his code for normal human emotions, like love and trust, just as there is no allowance for human imperfectibility. At the conclusion of their conversations, Joe is frustrated and disgusted; Jake feels stimulated, as he always does after a serious conversation: "Articulation! There, by Joe, was my absolute . . . to turn experience into speech—that is, to classify, to categorize, to conceptualize, to grammarize, to syntactify it—is always a betrayal of experience, a falsification of it; but only so betrayed can it be dealt with at all, and only in so dealing with it did I ever feel a man, alive and kicking" (112–13). When he thinks about it at all, he says, "I responded to . . . this adroit, careful mythmaking with all the upsetting exhilaration of any artist at his work." In other senses, however, he doesn't believe any of this.

As Jake admits, he can maintain "with perfect equal unenthusiasm contradictory . . . opinions at once on a given subject." He feels a whole range of contradictory emotions on the afternoon after Joe's visit. When Rennie comes up to his room, she asks him what he thinks of Joe and he says he has a number of opinions: he is noble, strong, brave, ridiculous, contemptible, a buffoon, a sophist, a boor, arrogant, small, intolerable, a little bit cruel and even stupid. He thinks all things can be solved by intelligence. Most of all, Jake says, "I think he is . . . a pretty remarkable guy, more pathetic than tragic and more amusing than contemptible." Jake asks her again why Joe sent her up there and her answer is predictible.

He has convinced her that regardless of how repulsive the idea may seem to her now, when she went to bed with Jake it was because she *wanted* to, that she believed it was all right for her to make love to Jake because she did. Her next statement flabbergasts even Jake, "He has sent me up here to do it again." He can only reply, "Joe's insane. You know I could say this strikes me as perverted on his part" (119).

Jake's relations with Rennie that fall make him more aware than ever of the inadequacy of Mythotherapy as a means of solving human problems:

> The trouble, I suppose, is that the more one learns about a given person, the more difficult it becomes to assign a character to him that will allow one to deal with him effectively in an emotional situation. Mythotherapy, in short, becomes increasingly harder to apply, because one is compelled to recognize the inadequacy of any role one assigns. Existence not only precedes essence: in the case of human beings it rather defies essence, and as soon as one knows a person well enough to hold contradictory opinions about him, Mythotherapy goes out the window, except at times when one is no more than half awake. (122)

Jake does not think the disintegration of Rennie is a pretty sight, and he is often not able to perform the role Joe had assigned him by reducing the whole matter to an abstraction. Joe considers it, Jake says, a "romantic conquest between symbols," Joe being "The Reason or Being" and "I . . . the Unreason or Not Being" and the two of them fighting, like God and the Devil, for the soul of Rennie. Rennie continues to come to Jake's, sometimes as emotionless as an automaton, sometimes with a zestfulness that seems to suggest that she is almost enjoying her ordeal. Sometimes even Rennie tries a little Mythotherapy, assigning different roles to the three participants in the drama—The Over-Zealous and Too Serious Husband, the Too Easily Swayed Housewife, and the Unambitious and Bored Bachelor.

In the wake of this allegorical clash, the novel moves rapidly to its close. One night Joe and Rennie visit Jake's room, bringing the .45 Colt revolver Joe has mentioned once before, and Joe announces that Rennie is pregnant. Joe says they don't know who is the father of the child. Jake immediately adopts the role suggested to him by this turn of events. He will be the Saviour who brings order out of chaos; consequently he makes an elaborate plan to get an abortionist, only to have Rennie say she won't go through with it because she is through lying. Then Jake seeks the help of Peggy Rankin and is flatly refused. She knows he's practicing Mythotherapy again. He makes arrangements for the Doctor at the farm to perform the abortion, and Rennie dies on the operating table. (He is not a physician; therefore he, too, is merely practicing Mythotherapy.) The Doctor's only comment is: "This thing was everybody's fault, Horner. Let it be everybody's lesson" (183).

No more devastating comment on the inadequacies of existentialism exists in modern literature. Man, it would seem, is destined to live in a meaningless world, one in which he is completely alienated and dehumanized. Joe Morgan oversimplifies a complex world in order to try to impose some degree of rational order on a basically irrational universe. Mythotherapy, which finds its origins in existentialism, is not effective when human beings are acting like human beings. Starting with basically the same set of assumptions, Percy and Barth reach opposite conclusions. Through a heightened awareness of the sensuous world around him—the result of his manually manipulating physical phenomena while he is engaged in a "horizontal search," Binx Bolling establishes deep personal relationships with Kate Cutrer and Lonnie Smith. He discovers the integrity and the transcendent nature of the human spirit. Beginning, as Percy did, with the principle that existence precedes essence, Barth ends with nihilism, nothing or nobody really exists. Human speculation on morals and ethics is of no consequence because mere existence precludes essence. He seems inclined to suggest only one positive virtue and that in a most tentative and cautious manner: human beings in some way may be responsible for the repercussions of their actions. The prospects for man, in a world devoid of *both* dogma and ritual, seem very bleak indeed, for only nothingness prevails.